LUDWIG WITTGENSTEIN

A MEMOIR

LUDWIG WITTGENSTEIN

A MEMOIR
by Norman Malcolm

.

with a Biographical Sketch
by G. H. von Wright

.

Second edition
*with Wittgenstein's letters
to Malcolm*

Oxford   New York
OXFORD UNIVERSITY PRESS
1984

Oxford University Press, Walton Street, Oxford OX2 6DP

London New York Toronto
Delhi Bombay Calcutta Madras Karachi
Kuala Lumpur Singapore Hong Kong Tokyo
Nairobi Dar es Salaam Cape Town
Melbourne Auckland

and associated companies in
Beirut Berlin Ibadan Mexico City Nicosia

Oxford is a trade mark of Oxford University Press

Biographical Sketch and Memoir first published 1958 by Oxford University Press
First issued as an Oxford University Press paperback 1962
Second edition, with Wittgenstein's letters to Malcolm, first published as
an Oxford University Press paperback 1984

British Library Cataloguing in Publication Data

Malcolm, Norman
Ludwig Wittgenstein.—2nd ed.—(Oxford paperbacks)
1. Wittgenstein, Ludwig   2. Philosophers—Austria—Biography
I. Title
192   B3376.W564
ISBN 0-19-283042-2

Library of Congress Cataloging in Publication Data

Malcolm, Norman, 1911–
Ludwig Wittgenstein: a memoir.
Includes index.
1. Wittgenstein, Ludwig, 1889–1951. 2. Philosophers—Germany—Biography.
I. Wright, G. H. von (Georg Henrik), 1916–. II. Title.
B3376.W564M2 1984   192 [B]   84-953
ISBN 0-19-283042-2 (pbk.)

Set by Promenade Graphics Ltd., Cheltenham
Printed in the United States of America

CONTENTS

PREFACE

TO THE

SECOND EDITION

This book comprises three parts: Georg Henrik von Wright's Biographical Sketch, my own Memoir, and the complete text of the letters that I received from Wittgenstein, together with my comments on these.

The Biographical Sketch first appeared in Swedish in 1954, in the yearbook of the Philosophical Society of Finland. An English version was published in the *Philosophical Review* the following year, and reprinted in 1958 in the first edition of the present book. Professor von Wright made a number of corrections and revisions for the 1967 reprint of that edition, and a few further changes in 1982, when the sketch was included as one of the essays in his *Wittgenstein*.

The most noteworthy feature of this new edition is the presentation in full of all the letters that I received from Wittgenstein over a period of eleven years (1940–51). They are handwritten and in English. In the printed version of the letters at the end of this book, and in the quotations from them in the Memoir, Wittgenstein's grammar, punctuation and spelling have been retained.

Although there are numerous quotations from the letters in the Memoir, it seems to me that the complete letters reveal some features of Wittgenstein's character and personality more vividly than is done by the Memoir alone. One sees from the letters how greatly friendships mattered to him, and how much he was concerned for the health and well-being of his friends. He sometimes cautioned, advised or even rebuked them, but the letters reveal how unpretentious he was: they show him joshing and making little jokes, and warmly affectionate. In a word, they disclose the *human* qualities of Wittgenstein better than anything else could do; therefore they are an appropriate complement to the Memoir.

The Memoir itself, first published in 1958, has undergone no previous revision. Its narrative aspect has been left untouched in this edition. The principal change has been to shorten a number of quotations in order to reduce duplication. The full texts of the letters are numbered, and the numbers in square brackets at the end of the quotations in the Memoir identify their source. At the end of the Memoir there are a few Additional Notes.

1984   N. M.

A BIOGRAPHICAL SKETCH

BY G. H. VON WRIGHT

ON 29 April 1951 there died at Cambridge one of the greatest and most influential philosophers of our time, Ludwig Wittgenstein.

It has been said that Wittgenstein inspired two important schools of thought, both of which he repudiated. The one is so-called logical positivism or logical empiricism, which played a prominent role during the decade immediately preceding the Second World War. The other is an even more heterogeneous trend which cannot be covered by *one* name. In its early phase it was sometimes called the Cambridge School of analysis. After the war its influence came to prevail at Oxford and the movement became known as linguistic philosophy, or the Oxford School.

It is true that the philosophy of Wittgenstein has been of great importance to both of these trends in contemporary thought: to the first, his early work *Tractatus Logico-Philosophicus* and discussions with some members of the Vienna Circle; to the second, besides the *Tractatus*, his lectures at Cambridge and also glimpses of the works which he did not publish in his lifetime. It is also partly true that Wittgenstein repudiated the results of his own influence. He did not participate in the worldwide discussion to which his work and thought had given rise. He was of the opinion—justified, I believe—that his ideas were usually misunderstood and distorted even by those who professed to be his disciples. He doubted that he would be better understood in the future. He once said that he felt as though he were writing for people who would think in a quite different way, breathe a different air of life, from that of present-day men. For people of a different culture, as it were.[1] That was *one* reason why he did not himself publish his later works.

Wittgenstein avoided publicity. He withdrew from every contact with his surroundings that he thought undesirable. Outside the circle of his family and personal friends, very little was known about his life and character. His inaccessibility contributed to absurd legends about his personality and to widespread misunderstandings of his teaching. The data published in his obituaries have often

[1] See his Foreword to *Philosophische Bemerkungen* (*Philosophical Remarks*) and my essay 'Wittgenstein in Relation to his Times' in *Wittgenstein* (Blackwell, Oxford, 1982), pp. 201–16.

been erroneous and the atmosphere of most biographical articles on Wittgenstein that I have read has been alien to their subject.

Ludwig Josef Johann Wittgenstein was born in Vienna on 26 April 1889. The Wittgenstein family had migrated from Saxony to Austria. It is of Jewish descent. It is not, contrary to what has often been stated, related to the house of princes of the same name. Wittgenstein's grandfather was a convert from the Jewish religion to Protestantism. His mother was a Roman Catholic. Ludwig Wittgenstein was baptized in the Catholic Church.

Wittgenstein's father must have been a man of remarkable intelligence and will-power. He was an engineer who became a leading figure in the iron and steel industry of the Austro-Hungarian empire. Wittgenstein's mother was responsible for a strong artistic influence in the family. Both she and her husband were highly musical. The wealthy and cultured home of the Wittgensteins became a centre of musical life. Johannes Brahms was a close friend of the family.

Ludwig was the youngest of five brothers and three sisters. Nature was lavish to all the children both in respect of character and of artistic and intellectual talents. Ludwig Wittgenstein was undoubtedly a most uncommon man. Though he was free from that form of vanity which shows itself in a desire to seem different, it was inevitable that he should stand out sharply from his surroundings. It is probably true that he lived on the border of mental illness. A fear of being driven across it followed him throughout his life. But it would be wrong to say of his work that it had a morbid character. It is deeply original but not at all eccentric. It has the same naturalness, frankness, and freedom from all artificiality that was characteristic of him.

Wittgenstein was educated at home until he was 14. For three years thereafter he was at a school at Linz in Upper Austria. It seems to have been his wish to study physics with Boltzmann in Vienna. However, Boltzmann died in 1906, the same year that Wittgenstein finished school. Wittgenstein proceeded to the Technische Hochschule in Berlin-Charlottenburg.

That he chose to study engineering was a consequence of his early interests and talents, rather than of his father's influence. Throughout his life he was extremely interested in machinery. While a small boy he constructed a sewing machine that aroused much admiration. Even in his last years he would spend a whole day with his beloved steam-engines in the South Kensington

Museum. There are several anecdotes of his serving as a mechanic when machinery that was out of order needed mending.

Wittgenstein remained in Berlin until the spring of 1908. Then he went to England. In the summer of 1908 he was experimenting with kites at the Kite Flying Upper Atmosphere Station, near Glossop, in Derbyshire. The same autumn he registered as a research student in the department of engineering at the University of Manchester. He was registered there until the autumn of 1911, but spent substantial periods on the Continent. During those years he was occupied with research in aeronautics. From his kite-flying experiments he passed on to the construction of a jet reaction propeller for aircraft. At first it was the engine that absorbed his interest, but soon he concentrated on the design of the propeller, which was essentially a mathematical task. It was at this time that Wittgenstein's interests began to shift, first to pure mathematics and then to the foundations of mathematics.

Wittgenstein once mentioned to me that the problems on which he worked during his Manchester years had since become very urgent. I regret that I was not curious enough to ask him more. I assume that he was thinking of the role which the reaction engine has come to play, especially in aeronautics.[2]

In Wittgenstein's life the years from 1906 to 1912 were a time of painful seeking and of final awakening to clarity about his vocation. He told me that in those years he was constantly unhappy. To his restlessness bear witness the several interruptions of work already begun and the flights to something new: the departure from Germany to England, the experiments with kites, the construction of the jet engine, the design of the propeller, the interest in pure mathematics and finally in the philosophy of mathematics.

It is said that Wittgenstein asked someone for advice about literature on the foundations of mathematics and was directed to Bertrand Russell's *Principles of Mathematics*, which had appeared in 1903. It seems clear that this book profoundly affected Wittgenstein's development, and was probably what led him to study the works of Frege. The 'new' logic which in Frege and Russell had two

[2] Data about Wittgenstein's time at Manchester have been recorded by Mr. W. Eccles and Mr. W. Mays. The design of the reaction engine and a number of other documents relating to this period in Wittgenstein's life have been deposited in the University Library at Manchester. I am told that Wittgenstein had patented some of his inventions in the field of aeronautics.

of its most brilliant representatives became the gateway through which Wittgenstein entered philosophy.

If I remember rightly,[3] Wittgenstein told me that he had read Schopenhauer's *Die Welt als Wille und Vorstellung* in his youth and that his first philosophy was a Schopenhauerian epistemological idealism. I know nothing of how this interest was related to his interest in logic and the philosophy of mathematics, except that I remember his saying that it was Frege's conceptual realism which made him abandon his earlier idealistic views.

Having decided to give up his studies in engineering, Wittgenstein first went to Jena in Germany to discuss his plans with Frege. It was apparently Frege who advised Wittgenstein to go to Cambridge and study with Russell. He followed the advice.[4]

This was probably in the autumn of 1911.[5] At the beginning of the following year he was admitted to Trinity College and registered in the University, first as an undergraduate and later as an 'advanced student'. He was at Cambridge for all three terms of the year 1912 and the first two terms of 1913. At the beginning of the autumn of 1913 he visited Norway with David Pinsent, a young mathematician with whom he had made friends at Cambridge. After a short visit to England in October, he returned to Norway alone and took up residence on a farm at Skjolden in Sogn, northeast of Bergen. Here he lived for most of the time until the outbreak of war in 1914. He liked the people and the country very much and eventually learned to speak Norwegian fairly well. In an isolated place near Skjolden he built himself a hut, where he could live in complete seclusion.

The decade before the First World War was a period of exceptional intellectual activity at Cambridge. Bertrand Russell had

[3] The biographical information I acquired from conversations with Wittgenstein I did not record on paper until after his death. I felt very strongly that it would have been improper to write them down following our conversations. He did not often talk about his past and only rarely of his youth, which was to him a painful recollection. The idea that someone was collecting data for a biography would certainly have been deeply distasteful to him.

[4] This is how Wittgenstein related the matter to me. His account is confirmed by notes made by his sister Hermine. Russell seems, therefore, to be mistaken when in his memorial article in *Mind*, NS lx (1951) he says that Wittgenstein had not known Frege before he came to Cambridge.

[5] I have not been able to fix the exact dates of Wittgenstein's first visit to Frege and arrival at Cambridge. He was registered at Manchester for the Michaelmas term of 1911.

arrived at the summit of his powers. He and A. N. Whitehead wrote *Principia Mathematica*, a milestone in the history of logic. The most influential philosopher was G. E. Moore. Wittgenstein soon became intimate with Russell,[6] and he saw much of Moore and Whitehead. Among Wittgenstein's friends during his early years at Cambridge should also be mentioned J. M. Keynes, the economist, G. H. Hardy, the mathematician, and the logician W. E. Johnson. Wittgenstein's *Tractatus* is dedicated to the memory of David Pinsent, who fell in the war.

Besides philosophy Wittgenstein did some experimental work in psychology at Cambridge. He carried out an investigation at the psychological laboratory concerning rhythm in music. He had hoped that the experiments would throw light on some questions of aesthetics that interested him. Wittgenstein was exceptionally musical, even if judged by the highest standards. He played the clarinet, and for a time he wished to become a conductor. He had a rare talent for whistling. It was a great pleasure to hear him whistle through a whole concerto, interrupting himself only to draw the listener's attention to some detail of the musical texture.

An important source of our knowledge of Wittgenstein during these years is a series of letters he wrote to Russell. Another is Pinsent's diary of their Cambridge life and their travels to Iceland and Norway. The letters and the diary help to illuminate Wittgenstein's personality, not only as a young man, but also as he appeared to his friends of the 1930s and 1940s. The letters also contain interesting information about the gradual development of the work that first established Wittgenstein's fame as a philosopher.

Wittgenstein's earliest philosophical investigations were in the realm of the problems with which Frege and Russell had dealt. Concepts such as 'propositional function', 'variable', 'generality', and 'identity' occupied his thoughts. He soon made an interesting discovery, a new symbolism for so-called 'truth-functions' that led to the explanation of logical truth as 'tautology'.[7]

The oldest parts of the *Tractatus* are those dealing with logic. Wittgenstein had formed his principal thoughts on these matters before the outbreak of war in 1914, and thus before his twenty-sixth

---

[6] Russell wrote in his memorial article in *Mind*: 'Getting to know Wittgenstein was one of the most exciting intellectual adventures of my life.'

[7] The symbolism in question is much the same as that explained in *Tractatus* 6.1203. The now familiar truth-tables (*Tractatus* 4.31 etc.) he invented later.

year. Later he became engrossed in a new problem. It was the question of the nature of the significant proposition.[8] There is a story of how the idea of language as a picture of reality occurred to Wittgenstein.[9] It was in the autumn of 1914, on the Eastern Front. Wittgenstein was reading in a magazine about a lawsuit in Paris concerning an automobile accident. At the trial a miniature model of the accident was presented before the court. The model here served as a proposition; that is, as a description of a possible state of affairs. It has this function owing to a correspondence between the parts of the model (the miniature-houses, -cars, -people) and things (houses, cars, people) in reality. It now occurred to Wittgenstein that one might reverse the analogy and say that a *proposition* serves as a model or *picture*, by virtue of a similar correspondence between *its* parts and the world. The way in which the parts of the proposition are combined—the *structure* of the proposition—depicts a possible combination of elements in reality, a possible state of affairs.

Wittgenstein's *Tractatus* may be called a synthesis of the theory of truth-functions and the idea that language is a picture of reality. Out of this synthesis arises a third main ingredient of the book, its doctrine of that which cannot be *said*, only *shown*.

At the outbreak of war, Wittgenstein entered the Austrian army as a volunteer, although he had been exempted from service because of a rupture. He served first on a vessel on the Vistula and then in an artillery workshop at Cracow. Later he fought on the Eastern Front. In 1916 he was ordered to Olmütz, in Moravia, to be trained as an officer. In 1918 he was transferred to the Southern Front. Upon the collapse of the Austro-Hungarian army in October, he was taken prisoner by the Italians. It was not until August of the following year that he could return to Austria. During the major part of his captivity, he was in a prison camp near Monte Cassino, in southern Italy.

---

[8] 'My *whole* task consists in explaining the nature of the proposition', he wrote in one of the philosophical notebooks that he kept during the war.

[9] There exist several somewhat different versions of it. The story as told here is based on an entry in Wittgenstein's philosophical notebooks in June 1930. It would be interesting to know whether Wittgenstein's conception of the proposition as a picture is connected in any way with the Introduction to Heinrich Hertz's *Die Prinzipen der Mechanik*. Wittgenstein knew this work and held it in high esteem. There are traces of the impression that it made on him both in the *Tractatus* and in his later writings.

When Wittgenstein was captured he had in his rucksack the manuscript of his *Logisch-philosophische Abhandlung*, which is generally known by the Latin title proposed for it by G. E. Moore, *Tractatus Logico-Philosophicus.* He had completed the work when on a leave of absence, in August 1918. While still in captivity he got in touch with Russell by letter and was able to send the manuscript to him, thanks to the aid of one of his friends of the Cambridge years, Keynes. He also sent Frege a copy and corresponded with him.

It was Wittgenstein's habit to write down his thoughts in notebooks. The entries are usually dated, and thus they comprise a sort of diary. The contents of an earlier notebook are often worked over again in a later one. Sometimes he dictated to colleagues and pupils. In the spring of 1914 he dictated some thoughts on logic to Moore in Norway. In the late 1920s and the early 1930s he dictated to Schlick and Waismann. The so-called Blue Book was dictated in conjunction with lectures at Cambridge in the academic year 1933–4. The so-called Brown Book was dictated privately to some pupils in 1934–5.[10]

Several of the notebooks which led up to the *Tractatus* have been preserved.[11] These sketches and fragments of earlier versions are of great interest, partly because they show the development of his thoughts, partly because they illuminate many difficult passages in the extremely compressed final version. I have been especially impressed by a notebook of the year 1916. It deals chiefly with the ego, the freedom of the will, the meaning of life, and death. Thus the somewhat aphoristic remarks on these topics in the *Tractatus* are sifted from a quantity of material. The notes show how strong were the impressions that Wittgenstein had received from Schopenhauer. An occasional Spinozistic flavour is also recognizable.

In the earliest notebooks a considerable part of the content is written in a code. Wittgenstein continued to use this code throughout his life. The notes in code are for the most part of a personal nature.

The period of the war was a crisis in Wittgenstein's life. To what extent the turmoil of the time and his experiences in war and

---

[10] These two books were published in 1958 under the title *Preliminary Studies for the 'Philosophical Investigations', generally known as The Blue and Brown Books* (Blackwell, Oxford; 2nd edn. 1969).

[11] Published in 1961 under the title *Notebooks 1914–1916* (Blackwell, Oxford: 2nd edn. 1979).

captivity contributed to the crisis, I cannot say. A circumstance of
great importance was that he became acquainted with the ethical
and religious writings of Tolstoy. Tolstoy exercised a strong
influence on Wittgenstein's view of life, and also led him to study
the Gospels.

After the death of his father in 1912 Wittgenstein was in pos-
session of a great fortune. One of his first steps after his return from
the war was to give away all his money.[12] Henceforth a great simplicity, at times even an extreme frugality, became characteristic
of his life. His dress was unconventional; it is impossible to
imagine him with tie or hat. A bed, a table, and a few deckchairs
were all he had of furniture. Ornamental objects of whatever kind
were banished from his surroundings.

After the war Wittgenstein took up the vocation of schoolmaster. In 1919–20 he was trained at a college for teachers in elementary schools (*Lehrerbildungsanstalt*) in Vienna. From 1920 to 1926
he taught in various remote villages in the districts of Schneeberg
and Semmering in Lower Austria. This suited his wish for a simple
and secluded life. In other ways it did not suit him well. It appears
that he was in constant friction with the people around him.
Finally there was a serious crisis. Wittgenstein resigned his post
and quitted for ever the career of schoolmaster. He went to work as
a gardener's assistant with the monks at Hütteldorf, near Vienna.

In this period, Wittgenstein contemplated entering a monastery.
The same thought occurred to him at other times in his life too.
That it never came true was, partly at least, because for him the
inner conditions of monastic life were not satisfied.

His service with the monks soon came to an end. In the autumn
of 1926 Wittgenstein accepted a task that absorbed his time and
genius for two years. He built a mansion in Vienna for one of his
sisters. In the beginning he co-operated with his friend, the architect Paul Engelmann. But soon Wittgenstein took over entirely.
The building is his work down to the smallest detail and is highly
characteristic of its creator. It is free from all decoration and

---

[12] Before the war Wittgenstein had made a large anonymous grant for the pro-
motion of literature. Two poets of whom he was in this manner a benefactor
were Georg Trakl and Rainer Maria Rilke. (For more details see Ludwig Ficker's
article 'Rilke und der unbekannte Freund', in *Der Brenner*, 1954). It may be
remarked in passing that Wittgenstein had a high opinion of Trakl's talent, but
that later in life, at least, he did not greatly admire Rilke, whose poetry he
thought artificial.

marked by a severe exactitude in measure and proportion. Its beauty is of the same simple and static kind that belongs to the sentences of the *Tractatus*. It does not seem to me that the building can be classified as belonging to some one style. But the horizontal roofs and the materials—concrete, glass, and steel—remind the spectator of typically 'modern' architecture.[13] (In 1914 Wittgenstein had come to know Adolf Loos, whose work he admired.)

During this same period Wittgenstein executed a sculpture in the studio of his friend, the sculptor Drobil. It is the head of a young woman. The features have the same finished and restful beauty one finds in Greek sculptors of the classical period and which seems to have been Wittgenstein's ideal. In general, there is a striking contrast between the restlessness, the continual searching and changing, in Wittgenstein's life and personality, and the perfection and elegance of his finished work.

The author of the *Tractatus* thought he had solved all philosophical problems. It was consistent with this view that he should give up philosophy.

The publication of the book was largely due to Russell. In 1919 the two friends met in Holland to discuss the manuscript. The problem of finding a publisher caused difficulties and the matter was further complicated by Wittgenstein's strong disapproval of Russell's Introduction to the book. In July 1920 Wittgenstein wrote to Russell that he himself would take no further steps to have it published and that Russell could do with it as he wished. The German text was published in 1921 in the last issue of Ostwald's *Annalen der Naturphilosophie*. In the following year it was published in London with a parallel English translation.

During his years as schoolmaster and architect, Wittgenstein was not completely cut off from contact with the philosophical world. In 1923 a young man from Cambridge, Frank Ramsey, visited him at Puchberg, where he was then teaching. Ramsey had assisted in the translation of the *Tractatus* and had written, at the age of 20, a remarkably penetrating review of the book for *Mind*. The visit was repeated a year later. Ramsey tried to persuade

[13] Later the house was threatened by destruction. The garden adjoining it was vandalized and the house eventually sold to the state of Bulgaria. For a history and description of the building in its original shape, see Bernhard Leitner, *The Architecture of Ludwig Wittgenstein, A Documentation with Excerpts from the Family Recollections by Hermine Wittgenstein* (Press of the Nova Scotia College of Art and Design, Chatham, England, 1973).

Wittgenstein to come to England on a visit. He was helped in his efforts by Keynes, who even procured money for the purpose. In the summer of 1925 Wittgenstein finally did visit his English friends.

After Ramsey, Moritz Schlick, a professor in Vienna, managed to establish contact with Wittgenstein. The study of the latter's book had made a deep impression on this honest and intelligent man, who was to become famous as the founder and leader of the Vienna Circle. Wittgenstein's influence on the philosophical movement which the Vienna Circle started is thus in part due to a personal connection, lasting for a number of years, between Wittgenstein and Schlick. Another member of the Circle who was personally strongly influenced by Wittgenstein was Friedrich Waismann.

Wittgenstein said that he returned to philosophy because he felt that he could again do creative work. An external circumstance of this important step may have been that in March of 1928 he had heard Brouwer lecture in Vienna on the foundations of mathematics. It is rumoured to have been this which stirred him to take up philosophy again.[14] Early in 1929 Wittgenstein arrived at Cambridge. He was first registered as a research student, a somewhat unusual status for a man whom many already regarded as one of the foremost living representatives of his subject. The idea was that he should work for a Ph.D. It turned out, however, that he could count his pre-war residence at Cambridge as credit towards the degree and could present his book, published eight years earlier, as a thesis. He received his degree in June 1929. The following year he was made a Fellow of Trinity College.

Soon after his return to Cambridge Wittgenstein began to write down philosophical thoughts. His output in the years 1929–32 was, as always from then on, tremendous. From the manuscript notebooks he sifted remarks for two bulky typescripts. One is called *Philosophische Bemerkungen* (*Philosophical Remarks*); for the other he contemplated the names *Philosophische Betrachtungen* (*Philosophical Reflections*) or *Philosophische Grammatik* (*Philosophical Grammar*). They are virtually completed works.[15] But Wittgenstein did not publish them.

[14] Cf. Herbert Feigl, 'The Wiener Kreis in America', *Perspectives in American History* ii (Harvard University Press, 1968), p. 639.

[15] It was in reference to the *Philosophical Remarks* that Bertrand Russell, in 1930, reported to the Council of Trinity College, which was considering the award of a grant to Wittgenstein, as follows: 'The theories contained in this new work of Wittgenstein are novel, very original, and indubitably important.

The only philosophical writing that Wittgenstein himself published subsequent to the *Tractatus* was the paper 'Some Remarks on Logical Form'.[16] This paper was supposed to have been read by him to the annual meeting of British philosophers—the Joint Session of the Mind Association and the Aristotelian Society—in 1929. The papers prepared for these meetings are printed and distributed to the participants in advance, and are subsequently collected in a Supplementary Volume to the Proceedings of the Aristotelian Society. Wittgenstein surprised his audience by talking to them on an entirely different topic—the notion of the infinite in mathematics—and not reading his paper at all. Wittgenstein himself thought this paper worthless.

Wittgenstein's writings of the period anterior to the Blue Book are of considerable interest, not least to the historian of philosophical ideas. Their intrinsic value is, I think, less than that of either the *Tractatus* or the *Philosophical Investigations*. This is natural, considering that they represent a transitional stage in Wittgenstein's development.

It will probably remain a matter of future debate to what extent there is continuity between the 'early' Wittgenstein of the *Tractatus* and the 'later' Wittgenstein of the *Investigations*. The writings from 1929 to 1932 testify to a continuous development and struggle—out of the former work and in the direction of the later. The Blue Book of 1933–4 conveys more the impression of a first, still somewhat rough version of a radically new philosophy. I myself find it difficult to fit the Blue Book into the development of Wittgenstein's thoughts. The Brown Book is a somewhat different case. It may be regarded as a preliminary version of the beginning of the *Investigations*. In August 1936 Wittgenstein began a revision, in German, of the Brown Book which had been dictated in English one year earlier. He called the revision *Philosophische Untersuchungen* (*Philosophical Investigations*). He soon abandoned work

Whether they are true, I do not know. As a logician, who likes simplicity, I should wish to think that they are not, but from what I have read of them I am quite sure that he ought to have an opportunity to work them out, since when completed they may easily prove to constitute a whole new philosophy.' (Quoted with the permission of Lord Russell and the Council of Trinity College, Cambridge.)

[16] While he was a schoolmaster he published a German glossary for elementary schools, *Wörterbuch für Volks-und Bürgerschulen* (Holder-Piehler-Tempsky, Vienna, 1926).

on it as unsatisfactory, and made a fresh start in the autumn of the same year. What he then wrote is substantially identical with the first 188 sections of the *Investigations* in its printed form.

The young Wittgenstein had learned from Frege and Russell. His problems were in part theirs. The later Wittgenstein, in my view, has no ancestors in the history of thought. His work signals a radical departure from previously existing paths of philosophy.[17] But his problems grew to a great extent out of the *Tractatus*. This, I think, is the reason why Wittgenstein wanted the work which embodied his new philosophy to be printed together with the work of his youth.[18]

It is sometimes said that the later Wittgenstein resembles Moore. This is hardly true. Moore's and Wittgenstein's ways of thinking are in fact utterly different. Although their friendship lasted until the latter's death, I do not believe that there is any trace of an influence of Moore's philosophy on Wittgenstein. What Wittgenstein appreciated was Moore's intellectual vitality, his love of truth and freedom from vanity.

Of great importance in the origination of Wittgenstein's new ideas was the criticism to which his earlier views were subjected by two of his friends. One was Ramsey, whose premature death in 1930 was a heavy loss to contemporary thought. The other was Piero Sraffa, an Italian economist who had come to Cambridge shortly before Wittgenstein returned there. It was above all Sraffa's acute and forceful criticism that compelled Wittgenstein to abandon his earlier views and set out upon new roads. He said that his

---

[17] I have seen this statement, and the one preceding it, contested. But I think they are substantially correct and also important. The *Tractatus* belongs in a definite tradition in European philosophy, extending back beyond Frege and Russell at least to Leibniz. Wittgenstein's so-called 'later philosophy', as I see it, is quite different. Its *spirit* is unlike anything I know in Western thought and in many ways opposed to aims and methods in traditional philosophy. This is not incompatible with the fact—about which more is known now than when this essay was first published—that many of Wittgenstein's later ideas have *seeds* in works which he had read and conversations he had with others. It is interesting to note what Wittgenstein himself says about this in *Vermischte Bemerkungen* (edited by G. H. von Wright and translated into English by Peter Winch as *Culture and Value*, Blackwell, Oxford, 1980), especially pp. 18ff. and 36. In the latter place he says: 'I believe that my originality (if that is the right word) is an originality belonging to the soil rather than to the seed. (Perhaps I have no seed of my own.) Sow a seed in my soil and it will grow differently than it would in any other soil.'

[18] See the Preface to *Philosophical Investigations*.

discussions with Sraffa made him feel like a tree from which all branches had been cut. That this tree could become green again was due to its own vitality. The later Wittgenstein did not receive an inspiration from outside like that which the earlier Wittgenstein obtained from Frege and Russell.

From 1929 until his death, Wittgenstein lived—with some interruptions—in England. He became a British subject when, after the *Anschluss*, he had to give up his Austrian passport and make a choice between German and British nationality. But in general he was not fond of English ways of life and he disliked the academic atmosphere of Cambridge. When his Fellowship at Trinity College expired in 1935,[19] he had plans for settling in the Soviet Union. He visited Moscow and Leningrad in September and apparently was pleased with the visit. He did not go back, however, and from what he told me, I understood that the harshening of the political conditions in the Soviet Union in the mid-thirties had influenced his plans.[20] So Wittgenstein remained at Cambridge until the end of the academic year 1935–6. In the summer of 1936 he withdrew, after a holiday in France, to his hut in Norway. He stayed there, with an interruption around Christmas 1936, to nearly the end of the following year. In 1938 he returned to Cambridge. One year later he was elected to be Moore's successor in the chair of philosophy.

From the beginning of 1930 Wittgenstein lectured at Cambridge. As might be expected, his lectures were highly 'unacademic'.[21] He nearly always held them in his own room or in the college rooms of a friend. He had no manuscript or notes. He *thought* before the class. The impression was of a tremendous concentration. The exposition usually led to a question, to which the audience were supposed to suggest an answer. The answers in turn became starting points for new thoughts leading to new questions. It depended on the audience, to a great extent, whether the discussion became

[19] The Fellowship was prolonged to include the whole of the academic year 1935–6. When he became a professor, Wittgenstein was again made a Fellow of Trinity College.

[20] Fania Pascal doubts that thought of the political developments in the Soviet Union influenced Wittgenstein's plans. See her essay 'Wittgenstein: A Personal Memoir', in Rush Rhees (ed.), *Recollections of Wittgenstein* (Oxford University Press, 1984), pp. 29ff. and pp. 41ff.

[21] A vivid and accurate impression of Wittgenstein as a teacher is conveyed by the memorial article, signed D.A.T.G.–A.C.J., in *Australasian Journal of Philosophy* xxix (1951).

fruitful and whether the connecting thread was kept in sight from the beginning to end of a lecture and from one lecture to another. Many members of his audiences were highly qualified people in their various fields. Moore attended Wittgenstein's lectures for some years in the early 1930s.[22] Several of those who later became leading philosophers in England, the United States, or Australia heard Wittgenstein lecture at Cambridge. There exist good, more or less verbatim notes of some of his lecture courses.

Before Wittgenstein assumed his chair, the Second World War broke out. I think one may say that he wished for the war. But, as in 1914, he did not want to watch it from an ivory tower. For some time he served as a porter at Guy's Hospital in London. Later he worked in a medical laboratory at Newcastle. It should be mentioned that Wittgenstein had been strongly attracted to the medical profession and that once in the 1930s he seriously considered leaving philosophy to take up medicine. During his time at Newcastle he devised some technical innovations that proved useful.

It need not surprise us that Wittgenstein's restless genius was not happy in academic routine. It is likely that if the war had not come his tenure of the chair would have been even briefer. In the Easter term of 1947 he gave his last lectures at Cambridge. In the autumn he was on leave, and from the end of the year he ceased to be a professor. He wanted to devote all his remaining strength to his research. As so often before in his life, he went to live in seclusion. For the winter of 1948 he settled on a farm in the Irish countryside. After that he lived quite by himself in a hut beside the ocean, in Galway on the west coast of Ireland. His neighbours were primitive fishermen. It is said that Wittgenstein became a legend among his neighbours because he had tamed so many birds; they used to come every day to be fed by him. The life in Galway, however, became physically too strenuous for him, and in the autumn of 1948 he moved to a hotel in Dublin. From then until early spring of the following year he had an excellent working period. It was then he completed the second part of the *Investigations*.

During the last two years of his life Wittgenstein was severely ill. In the autumn of 1949 it was found that he suffered from cancer.

---

[22] Moore published a full account and an interesting discussion of these lectures in *Mind*, NS lxiii–lxiv (1954–5). Moore's articles can be said to be a commentary on some of the views that Wittgenstein held in the 'period of transition' (1929–33) preceding the Blue Book.

Wittgenstein was then on a visit to Cambridge after his return from a stay in the United States. He did not go back to Ireland, but remained with friends in Oxford and in Cambridge. In the autumn of 1950 he visited Norway with a friend and even had plans for settling there again at the beginning of the following year. During part of his illness he was incapable of work. But it is remarkable that during the last two months he was not in bed and was apparently in the best of spirits. As late as two days before his death he wrote down thoughts that are equal to the best he produced.

Wittgenstein's very unusual and forceful personality exerted a great influence over others. No one who came in touch with him could fail to be impressed. Some were repelled. Most were attracted or fascinated. One can say that Wittgenstein avoided making acquaintances, but needed and sought friendships. He was an incomparable, but demanding, friend. I believe that most of those who loved him and had his friendship also feared him.

Just as there were many groundless legends concerning Wittgenstein's life and personality, so there grew up much unsound sectarianism among his pupils. This caused Wittgenstein much pain. He thought that his influence as a teacher was, on the whole, harmful to the development of independent minds in his disciples. I am afraid that he was right. And I believe that I can partly understand why it should be so. Because of the depth and originality of his thinking, it is very difficult to understand Wittgenstein's ideas and even more difficult to incorporate them into one's own thinking. At the same time the magic of his personality and style was most inviting and persuasive. To learn from Wittgenstein without coming to adopt his forms of expression and catchwords and even to imitate his tone of voice, his mien and gestures was almost impossible. The danger was that the thoughts should deteriorate into a jargon. The teaching of great men often has a simplicity and naturalness which makes the difficult appear easy to grasp. Their disciples usually become, therefore, insignificant epigones. The historical significance of such men does not manifest itself in their disciples but through influences of a more indirect, subtle, and often unexpected kind.

Wittgenstein's most characteristic features were his great and pure seriousness and powerful intelligence. I have never met a man who impressed me so strongly in either respect.

It seems to me that there are two forms of seriousness of character. One is fixed in 'strong principles'; the other springs from a passionate heart. The former has to do with morality and the latter, I believe, is closer to religion. Wittgenstein was acutely and even painfully sensitive to considerations of duty, but the earnestness and severity of his personality were more of the second kind. Yet I do not know whether he can be said to have been 'religious' in any but a trivial sense of the word. Certainly he did not have a Christian faith. But neither was his view of life un-Christian, pagan, as was Goethe's. To say that Wittgenstein was not a pantheist is to say something important.[23] 'God does not reveal himself *in* the world', he wrote in the *Tractatus*. The thought of God, he said, was above all for him the thought of the fearful judge.

Wittgenstein had the conviction, he sometimes said, that he was doomed. His outlook was typically one of gloom. Modern times were to him a dark age.[24] His idea of the helplessness of human beings was not unlike certain doctrines of predestination.

Wittgenstein was not, strictly speaking, a learned man. His temperament was very different from that of the typical scholar. 'Cool objectivity' and 'detached meditation' are labels which do not suit him at all. He put his whole soul into everything he did. His life was a constant journey, and doubt was the moving force within him. He seldom looked back on his earlier positions, and when he did so it was usually to repudiate them.

Knowledge, for Wittgenstein, was intimately connected with doing. It is significant that his first studies were in the technical sciences. He had a knowledge of mathematics and physics not derived from extensive reading, but from a working familiarity with mathematical and experimental techniques. His many artistic interests had the same active and living character. He could design a house, make a sculpture, or conduct an orchestra. Perhaps he would never have achieved mastery in those fields. But he was no 'dilettante'. Every manifestation of his multidimensional spirit came from the same earnest drive to create.

Wittgenstein had done no systematic reading in the classics of philosophy. He could read only what he could wholeheartedly assi-

---

[23] This statement must be modified, but I do not know exactly how. From the *Notebooks 1914–1916* a view can be extracted which identifies God and the world, not unlike Spinoza's *Deus sive Natura*. I am here indebted to Brian McGuinness. Cf. his paper 'The Mysticism of the *Tractatus*', *Philosophica Review* lxxv (1966).

[24] See the Preface to *Philosophical Investigations*: 'the darkness of these times'.

milate. We have seen that as a young man he read Schopenhauer. From Spinoza, Hume, and Kant he said that he could only get occasional glimpses of understanding. I do not think that he could have enjoyed Aristotle or Leibniz, two great logicians before him. But it is significant that he did read and enjoy Plato. He must have recognized congenial features, both in Plato's literary and philosophical method and in the temperament behind the thoughts.

Wittgenstein received deeper impressions from some writers in the borderland between philosophy, religion, and poetry than from the philosophers, in the restricted sense of the word. Among the former are St Augustine, Kierkegaard, Dostoevsky, and Tolstoy. The philosophical sections of St Augustine's *Confessions* show a striking resemblance to Wittgenstein's own way of doing philosophy. Between Wittgenstein and Pascal there is a trenchant parallelism which deserves closer study. It should also be mentioned that Wittgenstein held the writings of Otto Weininger in high regard.

An aspect of Wittgenstein's work which is certain to attract growing attention is its language. It would be surprising if he were not one day ranked among the classic writers of German prose. The literary merits of the *Tractatus* have not gone unnoticed. The language of the *Investigations* is equally remarkable. The style is simple and perspicuous, the construction of sentences firm and free, the rhythm flows easily. The form is sometimes that of dialogue, with questions and replies; sometimes, as in the *Tractatus*, it condenses to aphorisms. There is a striking absence of all literary ornamentation, and of technical jargon or terminology. The union of measured moderation with richest imagination, the simultaneous impression of natural continuation and surprising turns, leads one to think of some other great productions of the genius of Vienna. (Schubert was Wittgenstein's favourite composer.)

It may appear strange that Schopenhauer, one of the masters of philosophical prose, did not influence Wittgenstein's style. An author, however, who reminds one, often astonishingly, of Wittgenstein is Lichtenberg. Wittgenstein esteemed him highly. To what extent, if any, he can be said to have learned from him I do not know. It is deserving of mention that some of Lichtenberg's thoughts on philosophical questions show a striking resemblance to Wittgenstein's.[25]

[25] See my paper 'Georg Christoph Lichtenberg als Philosoph', *Theoria* viii (1942).

It is fairly certain that both the work and personality of Wittgen-stein will provoke varying comments and different interpretations in the future. The author of the sentences 'The riddle does not exist' and 'Everything that can be said can be said clearly' was him-self an enigma, and his sentences have a content that often lies deep beneath the surface of the language. In Wittgenstein many contrasts meet. It has been said that he was at once a logician and a mystic. *Neither* term is appropriate, but each hints at something true. Those who approach Wittgenstein's work will sometimes look for its essence in a rational, matter-of-fact dimension, and sometimes more in a supra-empirical, metaphysical one. In the existing literature on Wittgenstein there are examples of both con-ceptions. Such 'interpretations' have little significance. They must appear as falsifications to anyone who tries to understand Wittgen-stein in all his rich complexity. They are interesting only as show-ing in how many directions his influence extends. I have sometimes thought that what makes a man's work *classic* is often just this multiplicity, which invites and at the same time resists our craving for clear understanding.

A MEMOIR

BY NORMAN MALCOLM

I FIRST saw Wittgenstein in the Michaelmas term of 1938, my first term at Cambridge. At a meeting of the Moral Science Club, after the paper for the evening was read and the discussion started, someone began to stammer a remark. He had extreme difficulty in expressing himself and his words were unintelligible to me. I whispered to my neighbour, 'Who is that?': he replied, 'Wittgenstein.' I was astonished, because, for one reason I had expected the famous author of the *Tractatus Logico-Philosophicus* to be an elderly man, whereas this man looked *young*—perhaps about 35. (His actual age was 49.) His face was lean and brown, his profile was aquiline and strikingly beautiful, his head was covered with a curly mass of brown hair. I observed the respectful attention that everyone in the room paid to him. After his unsuccessful beginning he did not speak for a time but was obviously struggling with his thoughts. His look was concentrated, he made striking gestures with his hands as if he were discoursing. All the others maintained an intent and expectant silence. I witnessed this phenomenon countless times thereafter and came to regard it as entirely natural.

I attended Wittgenstein's lectures, which were on the philosophical foundations of mathematics, in the Lent term of 1939. He continued on this topic in the Easter and Michaelmas terms of 1939. I think that I understood almost nothing of the lectures, until I restudied my notes approximately ten years later. Nevertheless I was aware, as others were, that Wittgenstein was doing something important. One knew that he was fighting his way through profoundly difficult problems and that his method of attacking them was absolutely original.

His lectures were given without preparation and without notes. He told me that once he had tried to lecture from notes but was disgusted with the result; the thoughts that came out were 'stale', or, as he put it to another friend, the words looked like 'corpses' when he began to read them. In the method that he came to use his only preparation for the lecture, as he told me, was to spend a few minutes before the class met, recollecting the course that the inquiry had taken at the previous meetings. At the beginning of the lecture he would give a brief summary of this and then he would start from there, trying to advance the investigation with fresh thoughts. He told me that the only thing that made it possible for him to conduct his lecture classes in this extemporaneous way was the fact that he had done and was doing a vast amount of thinking and writing about all the problems under discussion. This is undoubtedly true; nevertheless, what occurred in these class meetings was largely *new* research.

Whether lecturing or conversing privately, Wittgenstein always spoke emphatically and with a distinctive intonation. He spoke excellent English, with the accent of an educated Englishman, although occasional Germanisms would appear in his constructions. His voice was resonant, the pitch being somewhat higher than that of the normal male voice, but not unpleasant. His words came out, not fluently, but with great force. Anyone who heard him say anything knew that here was a singular person. His face was remarkably mobile and expressive when he talked. His eyes were deep and often fierce in their expression. His whole personality was commanding, even imperial.

In contrast, his dress was as simple as possible. He always wore light grey flannel trousers, a flannel shirt open at the throat, a woollen lumber jacket or a leather jacket. Out of doors, in wet weather, he wore a tweed cap and a tan raincoat. He nearly always walked with a light cane. One could not imagine Wittgenstein in a suit, necktie, or hat. His clothes, except the raincoat, were always extremely clean and his shoes polished. He was about five feet six inches in height and slender.

He met his class twice weekly for a two-hour meeting, from five to seven p.m. He demanded promptness and became angry if someone came in two minutes late. Before he was a professor the meetings were mainly held in the college rooms of various friends of his, and thereafter in his own rooms in Whewell's Court, Trinity College. Members of the class brought in chairs or sat on the floor. At times the jam was formidable. This was especially true of the lectures that began the Michaelmas term of 1946; for about thirty people turned up and were wedged together without an inch to spare.

Wittgenstein's rooms in Whewell's Court were austerely furnished. There was no easy chair or reading lamp. There were no ornaments, paintings, or photographs. The walls were bare. In his living-room were two canvas chairs and a plain wooden chair, and in his bedroom a canvas cot. An old-fashioned iron heating stove was in the centre of the living-room. There were some flowers in a window box, and one or two flower pots in the room. There was a metal safe in which he kept his manuscripts, and a card table on which he did his writing. The rooms were always scrupulously clean.

The chairs that members of the class brought in belonged to Trinity and were kept on the landing between lectures. If someone came late this involved a considerable disruption, because chairs already placed had to be moved to make room.

One had to be brave to enter after the lecture had begun, and some would go away rather than face Wittgenstein's glare.

Wittgenstein sat in a plain wooden chair in the centre of the room. Here he carried on a visible struggle with his thoughts. He often felt that he was confused, and said so. Frequently he said things like 'I'm a fool!', 'You have a dreadful teacher!', 'I'm just too stupid today.' Sometimes he expressed a doubt that he would be able to continue the lecture, but only rarely did he give up before seven o'clock.

It is hardly correct to speak of these meetings as 'lectures', although this is what Wittgenstein called them. For one thing, he was carrying on original research in these meetings. He was thinking about certain problems in a way that he could have done had he been alone. For another thing, the meetings were largely conversation. Wittgenstein commonly directed questions at various people present and reacted to their replies. Often the meetings consisted mainly of dialogue. Sometimes, however, when he was trying to draw a thought out of himself, he would prohibit, with a peremptory motion of the hand, any questions or remarks. There were frequent and prolonged periods of silence, with only an occasional mutter from Wittgenstein, and the stillest attention from the others. During these silences, Wittgenstein was extremely tense and active. His gaze was concentrated; his face was alive; his hands made arresting movements; his expression was stern. One knew that one was in the presence of extreme seriousness, absorption, and force of intellect.

Wittgenstein's personality dominated these meetings. I doubt that anyone in the class failed to be influenced by him in some way. Few of us could keep from acquiring imitations of his mannerisms, gestures, intonations, exclamations. These imitations could easily appear ridiculous when compared with their original.

Wittgenstein was a frightening person at these classes. He was very impatient and easily angered. If someone felt an objection to what he was saying he was fiercely insistent that the objection should be stated. Once when Yorick Smythies, an old friend of Wittgenstein's, was unable to put his objection into words, Wittgenstein said to him very harshly, 'I might as well talk to this stove!' Fear of Wittgenstein helped to keep our attention at a high pitch. This was a valuable result since the problems were of extreme difficulty and Wittgenstein's methods of examining them were enormously hard to understand. I was always conscious of the mental exertion required to follow him, and two hours of it was more than I was good for.

Wittgenstein's severity was connected, I think, with his passionate love of truth. He was constantly fighting with the deepest philosophical problems. The solution of one problem led to another problem. Wittgenstein was uncompromising; he had to have *complete* understanding. He drove himself fiercely. His whole being was under a tension. No one at the lectures could fail to perceive that he strained his will, as well as his intellect, to the utmost. This was one aspect of his absolute, relentless honesty. Primarily, what made him an awesome and even terrible person, both as a teacher and in personal relationships, was his ruthless integrity, which did not spare himself or anyone else.

Wittgenstein was always exhausted by his lectures. He was also revolted by them. He felt disgusted with what he had said and with himself. Often he would rush off to a cinema immediately after the class ended. As the members of the class began to move their chairs out of the room he might look imploringly at a friend and say in a low tone, 'Could you go to a flick?' On the way to the cinema Wittgenstein would buy a bun or cold pork pie and munch it while he watched the film. He insisted on sitting in the very first row of seats, so that the screen would occupy his entire field of vision, and his mind would be turned away from the thoughts of the lecture and his feelings of revulsion. Once he whispered to me 'This is like a shower bath!' His observation of the film was not relaxed or detached. He leaned tensely forward in his seat and rarely took his eyes off the screen. He hardly ever uttered comments on the episodes of the film and did not like his companion to do so. He wished to become totally absorbed in the film no matter how trivial or artificial it was, in order to free his mind temporarily from the philosophical thoughts that tortured and exhausted him. He liked American films and detested English ones. He was inclined to think that there *could not* be a decent English film. This was connected with a great distaste he had for English culture and mental habits in general. He was fond of the film stars Carmen Miranda and Betty Hutton. Before he came to visit me in America he demanded in jest that I should introduce him to Miss Hutton.

Some have thought that Wittgenstein's lectures were only for his friends and favourites. In fact he would admit anyone to his lectures. He required, however, that they should attend continuously and for a considerable period of time. He would not allow anyone to come for only one or two meetings. To one such request he replied, 'My lectures are not for tourists.' I have known two cases in which he allowed someone to come for one term only, but he was reluctant to give such permission. This was reasonable. It kept the lectures from being invaded by numbers of the curious. And it was true that one had to attend for quite a long time (at least three terms, I should say) before one could begin to get *any* grasp of what he was doing.

It did matter to him who was in his classes. He liked to discuss philosophical questions 'with friends'. It was important to him that there should be some 'friendly faces' in his classes. He often remarked that he liked a certain 'face' and he wanted that face to be there even if the person said nothing. During World War II, when he lectured on Saturdays, an American negro soldier was a member of the class. Wittgenstein remarked more than once what a friendly and good-natured face the man had, and how sorry he was when he ceased to come. Usually more than half of those who came to his first lecture in the autumn would discontinue attendance after five or six meetings, because they found the material unintelligible or uninteresting. The ten or fifteen persons who remained were, in contrast, extremely zealous in their attendance.

A curious thing, which I observed innumerable times, was that when Wittgenstein invented an example during his lectures in order to illustrate a point, he himself would grin at the absurdity of what he had imagined. But if any member of the class were to chuckle, his expression would change to severity and he would exclaim in reproof, 'No, no; I'm serious!' The imaginary events and circumstances were so odd and so far beyond the reach of natural possibility that he himself could not help being amused; yet the intention of the example, of course, was serious. Wittgenstein could not tolerate a facetious tone in his classes, the tone that is characteristic of philosophical discussion among clever people who have no serious purpose.

It is worth noting that Wittgenstein once said that a serious and good philosophical work could be written that would consist entirely of *jokes* (without begin facetious). Another time he said that a philosophical treatise might contain nothing but questions (without answers). In his own writing he made wide use of both. To give an example: 'Why can't a dog simulate pain? Is he too honest?' (*Philosophical Investigations*, § 250).

Wittgenstein got acquainted with members of his class by having them individually to tea. I received such an invitation in 1939. There was no small talk. The conversation was serious and interspersed with long silences. The only topic that I recall had to do with my future. Wittgenstein wished to persuade me to give up my plan to become a teacher of philosophy. He wondered whether I could not do some manual job instead, such as working on a ranch or farm. He had an abhorrence of academic life in general and of the life of a professional philosopher in particular. He believed that a normal human being could not be a university teacher and also an honest and serious person. Of Smythies he once said: 'He will never get a lectureship. He is too serious.' Wittgenstein could not stand the society of academic colleagues. Although a Fellow of Trinity, he did not dine in Hall. He told me that he had tried to do it (there is an anecdote to the effect that he was once reprimanded by the Vice-Master for not wearing a tie at the High Table) but was revolted by the artificiality of the conversation. He really *hated* all forms of affectation and insincerity.

Wittgenstein several times renewed the attempt to persuade me to give up philosophy as a profession. He commonly did this with other students of his.

Despite these efforts he actually made it possible for me to continue the study of philosophy at Cambridge for another six months. This came about in the following way: My funds were derived from a Harvard University fellowship that I had held for two years and which could not be renewed. In the summer of 1939 my money was gone and I was under the necessity of returning to the States. But I was eager to remain a while longer. I was excited by the ideas that were in circulation at Cambridge, and I thought that I had just begun to get a slight understanding of Wittgenstein's works, an understanding that I wished very much to improve. Once when I was with Wittgenstein I mentioned my reluctance to return to the States just then. He wanted to know all about it. He then said that he saw that I was 'charmed' by Cambridge philosophy and that it would be a pity if I went away in that condition. He meant that if I stayed and got to know more about Cambridge philosophy, then I should no longer be charmed by it—which, in his opinion, would be a good thing. He thought that *he* might be able to provide me with money sufficient to live on for the next six months. And so it turned out. He gave (not lent) me a sum in cash each month from August 1939 to January 1940, when I had to return to the States. The total amount that he gave me during that period was in the neighbourhood of eighty pounds. He would not consider a repayment.

In 1939 Wittgenstein used to call at my rooms frequently to get me to accompany him on walks. These were usually on Midsummer Common and beyond, along the river. He usually brought bread or sugar to feed the horses on the Common. A walk with Wittgenstein was very exhausting. Whatever we talked about, he turned his mind to it with great seriousness and intensity, and it was a formidable strain on me to keep up with his thoughts. He would walk in spurts, sometimes coming to a stop while he made some emphatic remark and looking into my eyes with his piercing gaze. Then he would walk rapidly for a few yards, then slow down, then speed up or come to a halt, and so on. And this uncertain ambulation was conjoined with the most exacting conversation! The freshness and depth of Wittgenstein's thinking, no matter what the topic, was highly demanding of his companion. His remarks were never *commonplace*.

When in very good spirits he would jest in a comical manner. This took the form of deliberately absurd or extravagant remarks uttered in a tone, and with a mien, of affected seriousness. On one walk he 'gave' to me each tree that we passed, with the reservation that I was not to cut it down or do anything to it, or prevent the previous owners from doing anything to it: with those reservations it was henceforth *mine*. Once when we were walking across Jesus Green at night, he pointed at Cassiopeia and said that it was a 'W' and that it meant *Wittgenstein*. I said that I thought it was an 'M' written upside down and that it meant *Malcolm*. He gravely assured me that I was wrong.

These light-hearted moments were comparatively infrequent. Most commonly his thoughts were sombre. He was constantly depressed, I think, by the impossibility of arriving at understanding in philosophy. But he was worried perhaps even more deeply by the stupidity and heartlessness that present themselves daily in the world in forms that command respect. Of the things that came to his attention in the normal passage of events, hardly any gave him pleasure and many produced in him an emotion that was not far from grief. Often as we walked together he would stop and exclaim 'Oh, my God!', looking at me almost piteously, as if imploring a divine intervention in human events.

One time when we were walking along the river we saw a news-vendor's sign which announced that the German government accused the British government of instigating a recent attempt to assassinate Hitler with a bomb. This was in the autumn of 1939. Wittgenstein said of the German claim: 'It would not surprise me at all if it were true.' I retorted that I could not believe that the top people in the British government would do such a thing. I meant that the British were too civilized and decent to attempt anything so underhand; and I added that such an act was incompatible with the British 'national character'. My remark made Wittgenstein extremely angry. He considered it to be a great stupidity and also an indication that I was not learning anything from the philosophical training that he was trying to give me. He said these things very vehemently, and when I refused to admit that my remark was stupid he would not talk to me any more, and soon after we parted. He had been in the habit of coming to my lodging in Chesterton Road to take me on a short walk with him before his bi-weekly lectures. After this incident he stopped that practice. As will be seen, he kept the episode in mind for several years.

In 1939, G. E. Moore read a paper to the Moral Science Club on an evening when Wittgenstein did not attend. Moore was attempting to prove in his paper that a person can *know* that he has such and such a sensation, e.g. pain. This was in opposition to the view, originating with Wittgenstein, that the concepts of knowledge and certainty have no application to one's own sensations (see *Philosophical Investigations*, § 246). Wittgenstein subsequently heard about Moore's paper and reacted like a war-horse. He came to Moore's at-home, on the following Tuesday. G. H. von Wright, C. Lewy, Smythies and myself were there, and perhaps one or two others. Moore re-read his paper and Wittgenstein immediately attacked it. He was more excited than I ever knew him to be in a discussion. He was full of fire and spoke rapidly and forcefully. He put questions to Moore but frequently did not give Moore a chance to answer. This went on for at least two hours, with Wittgenstein talking almost continuously, Moore getting in a very few remarks, and scarcely a word said by anyone else. Wittgenstein's brilliance and power were impressive and even frightening. When he was discussing this meeting with Smythies some days later, the latter suggested that Wittgenstein had been rude to Moore, in not allowing him to reply. Wittgenstein scoffed at this suggestion as preposterous. But when he next saw Moore he asked, 'Do you think I was rude to you in that discussion?'—to which Moore replied, 'Yes, you were.' I heard that Wittgenstein then made a stiff and reluctant apology.[1]

In the winter of 1939, Moore again read a paper to the Moral Science Club. During the discussion Wittgenstein made a criticism of Moore which I thought had overlooked part of Moore's point, and I expressed this in the discussion by saying that I did not believe that Wittgenstein's criticism had been 'fair' to Moore. Directly after the meeting ended, and while people were still standing about, Wittgenstein walked up to me and said, eyes blazing with anger, 'If you knew anything at all you would know that I am never unfair to anyone. This proves that you have understood absolutely nothing of my lectures.' He turned and walked away. I was thunderstruck.

That night or the next day I talked to Smythies about this incident and explained to him that I had not meant that Wittgenstein was cheating Moore, but merely that he had missed part of Moore's point. Within a day or two I suddenly became ill with flu. A young German friend of mine, Tom Rosenmeyer, was worried because there was no one to look after me, and knowing that Wittgenstein and I were close friends, went to tell Wittgenstein about it. He had never met Wittgenstein. When Wittgenstein opened the door of his room to Rosenmeyer's knock, the latter simply said, 'Malcolm is ill.' Wittgenstein's immediate reply was, 'Wait, I'll come.' The two came at once. Wittgenstein walked up to my bed and said to me rather severely, 'Smythies thinks that I misunderstood what you meant and if that is so I am sorry.' He then made a fuss of arranging the room more comfortably for me, and undertook to fetch me medicine and food. I felt very happy over this reconciliation. A week or so later I departed for the States. One of the last things that Wittgenstein said before I left was, 'Whatever else you do I hope that you won't marry a lady-philosopher!'

[1] After reading the above, Mr. Yorick Smythies informs me that it is his present recollection that the issue of 'rudeness' was first raised by Moore himself when he accidentally met Wittgenstein in the street, and that Wittgenstein thereafter discussed the matter with either Smythies or Lewy.

So in February 1940 I returned to the United States after one and
a half years in Cambridge. Wittgenstein and I kept up a correspondence. I knew that he was fond of detective magazines. They could
not be obtained in England during wartime and periodically I sent
some to him from America. He had a preference for a magazine
published by Street & Smith, each number of which contained
several short detective stories. Wittgenstein acknowledged the
arrival of a package of magazines, in a letter from Cambridge.

> Thanks awfully! I'm sure they're grand. My critical eye can see
> that without having read them, because my critical eye is an X-
> ray eye & can penetrate from 2 to 4000 pages. That's in fact how
> I get all my learning. Now please take it easy! One magazine a
> month is *ample*. If you send me more I won't have time to do any
> philosophy. Also please don't waste your money on mags for me,
> & see that *you* get enough to eat! [1]

In subsequent letters during and after the war he referred to detective magazines more than once:

> It'll be fine to get detective mags from you. There is a terrible
> scarcity of them now. My mind feels all underfed.

> They are *rich* in mental vitamins & calories.

> The one way in which the ending of Lend-Lease really hits me is
> by producing a shortage of detective mags in this country. I can
> only hope Lord Keynes will make this quite clear in Washington.
> For I say: if the U.S.A. won't give us detective mags we can't give
> them philosophy, & so America will be the loser in the end. See?
> [4, 19, 14]

He compared Street & Smith 'mags' with *Mind*, the international
philosophical journal:

> If I read your mags I often wonder how anyone can read 'Mind'
> with all its impotence & bankruptcy when they could read Street
> & Smyth mags. Well, everyone to his taste. [12]

Two and a half years later he repeated the comparison:

> Your mags are wonderful. How people can read Mind if they
> could read Street & Smith beats me. If philosophy has anything
> to do with wisdom there's certainly not a grain of that in Mind,
> & quite often a grain in the detective stories. [27]

Once Wittgenstein was so pleased with a detective story that he lent it to both Moore and Smythies and wished me to try to find out what else the author had written:

> It may sound crazy, but when I recently re-read the story I liked it again so much that I thought I'd really like to write to the author & thank him. If this is nuts, don't be surprised, for so am I. [29]

Wittgenstein warned me more than once, in his letters, against the temptations to dishonesty that would beset me as a university instructor. When I wrote that I had been awarded the Ph.D. in philosophy, he replied:

> Congratulations to your Ph.D.! And now: may you make good use of it! By that I mean: may you not cheat either yourself or your students. Because, unless I'm very much mistaken, *that's* what will be expected from you. And it will be *very* difficult not to do it, & perhaps impossible; & in this case: may you have the strength *to quit*. This ends today's sermon. . . . I wish you good, not necessarily clever, thoughts, & decency that won't come out in the wash. [3]

In the autumn of 1940 I became an instructor at Princeton, and Wittgenstein wrote:

> I wish you good luck; in particular with your work at the university. The temptation for you to cheat yourself will be *overwhelming* (though I don't mean more for you than for anyone else in your position.). *Only by a miracle* will you be able to do decent work in teaching philosophy. Please remember these words, even if you forget everything I've ever said to you; &, if you can help it, don't think that I'm a crank because nobody else will say this to you. [4]

The following summer I told him that Princeton would not re-appoint me for more than one more year and that I might enter the army, to which he answered:

> I am sorry—*honestly*—that you find you won't be able to teach at Princeton after next year. You know what my opinion of teaching philosophy is & I haven't changed it; but I'd like you to quit for the *right* reasons, not for the wrong ones. ('Right' & 'wrong' as *I* can see it.) I know you'll make a good soldier; still, I hope you

won't have to be one. I wish you could live quiet, in a sense, & be in a position to be kind & *understanding* to all sorts of human beings who *need* it! Because we all need this sort of thing very badly. [5]

In the spring of 1942 I resigned my Princeton instructorship and entered the Navy. For three years I wrote to Wittgenstein only infrequently. His replies were always prompt and affectionate. Once he sent me a paper-bound copy of Gottfried Keller's *Hadlaub*, saying:

I enclose a foul copy of a very wonderful German novel. I couldn't get a decent copy—at least I had no time to look for a better one. German books, as you can imagine, are very difficult to get these days. You may find it rather difficult to read, &, of course, you mayn't like it; but I hope you will. It's a sort of a Christmas present & I hope you won't mind it being so dirty. The advantage of this is that you can read it down in the engine-room without making it *more* dirty. If you find you like it I'll try to get you the book of which this is only one story. There are five of them called: 'Züricher Novellen', because they're all in some way connected with Zürich: Keller was a Swiss, & one of the greatest German *prose* writers. [6]

Wittgenstein wrote this letter in November of 1942 from Guy's Hospital in London, where he worked as an orderly for part of the war. During the next year two letters came from the Royal Victoria Infirmary in Newcastle-upon-Tyne, where he was employed in the Clinical Research Laboratory. In one he regrets that

for external & internal reasons I can't do philosophy, for that's the only work that's given me real satisfaction. No other work really bucks me up. I'm extremely busy now & my mind is kept occupied the whole time but at the end of the day I just feel tired & sad—Well, *perhaps* better times will come again. . . . I very rarely come to Cambridge now, about once every three months. I've given up my rooms in College. I'm supposed, of course, to come back there as a professor after the war, but I must say I can't quite imagine how I'll be able to do it. I wonder if I'll ever be able to teach philosophy again regularly. I rather think I shan't be able. [7]

Three months later he writes from the same place:

I'm still at my old work but may possibly leave here soon as my boss is going into the army & the whole research unit may brake up, or get another boss. I am feeling rather lonely here & may try to get to some place where I have someone to talk to. E.g. to Swansea where Rhees is a lecturer in philosophy. [8]

Probably a long time elapsed before I replied to Wittgenstein, because the next letter to me was written nearly a year later in November 1944. He was back at Trinity College, Cambridge. In this letter he revived the incident of our quarrel about the alleged British plot to assassinate Hitler:

Thanks for your letter, dated Nov. 12th, which arrived this morning. I was glad to get it. I thought you had almost forgotten me, or perhaps wished to forget me. I had a particular reason for thinking this. Whenever I thought of you I couldn't help thinking of a particular incident which seemed to me very important. You & I were walking along the river towards the railway bridge & we had a heated discussion in which you made a remark about 'national character' that shocked me by it's primitiveness. I then thought: what is the use of studying philosophy if all that it does for you is to enable you to talk with some plausibility about some abstruse questions of logic, etc., & if it does not improve your thinking about the important questions of everyday life, if it does not make you more conscientious than any . . . journalist in the use of the DANGEROUS phrases such people use for their own ends. You see, I know that it's difficult to think *well* about 'certainty', 'probability', 'perception', etc. But it is, if possible, still more difficult to think, or *try* to think, really honestly about your life & other peoples lives. And the trouble is that thinking about these things is *not thrilling*, but often downright nasty. And when it's nasty then it's *most* important.—Let me stop preaching. What I wanted to say was this: I'ld *very* much like to see you again; but if we meet it would be wrong to avoid talking about serious non-philosophical things. Being timid I don't like clashes, & particularly not with people I like. But I'ld rather have a clash than mere superficial talk.—Well, I thought that when you gradually ceased writing to me it was because you felt that if we were to dig down deep enough we wouldn't be able to see eye to eye in very serious matters. *Perhaps I was quite wrong.* But anyway, if we live to see each other again let's not shirk digging. You can't think decently if you don't want to hurt yourself. I know all about it because I'm a shirker. . . . Read this letter in a good spirit! *Good luck!* [9]

Six months later (May 1945) my ship came into Southampton and I obtained leave for thirty-five hours to pay a visit to Cambridge. I saw Wittgenstein in the afternoon and stayed to supper with him. My meeting with him was difficult and painful. He showed no cordiality at all. He did not even greet me. He merely nodded to me, rather grimly, and asked me to sit down (this was in his rooms in Whewell's Court, Trinity). We sat in silence for a long time. When he did begin to talk to me I could not grasp the meaning of his remarks, although I tried with all my might, and I very keenly had the feeling that during my years of naval service my mind had deteriorated. He was cold and severe the whole time. We were not in touch with one another at all. He prepared a supper for us. The *pièce de resistance* was powdered eggs. Wittgenstein asked me whether I cared for them, and, knowing how he valued sincerity, I told him that in truth I thought they were dreadful. He did not like this reply. He muttered something to the effect that if they were good enough for him they were good enough for me. Later he related this incident to Smythies, and (according to Smythies) Wittgenstein took my distaste for powdered eggs as a sign that I had become a snob.

The day after this meeting Wittgenstein received a letter from me which had been written a few weeks before and which was a reply to the letter from which I last quoted above. I think that I may have acknowledged that my remarks about 'national character' were foolish (for I had come to think this), and I must have expressed an appreciation of what he had said in his previous letter to me. In any case he immediately wrote a reply in which he said that had he received the letter 'before I saw you it would have made getting into contact with you rather easier'. He adds:

I imagine there was a lot on *your* mind as well as on mine when you were with me. If you write to me, as I hope you will, you might call me by my Christian name & let me do the same. In case this should seem silly, or somehow wrong, to you, just say so frankly. I shan't be hurt. [10]

In a letter written a month later I spoke of the war as a 'boredom', to which he replied:

I want to say something about the war being a 'boredom'. If a boy

said that school was an intensive boredom one might answer
him that, if he only could get himself to learn what can really be
learned there, he would not find it *so* boring. Now forgive me for
saying that I can't help believing that an enormous lot can be
learnt about human beings in this war—*if* you keep your eyes
open. And the better you are at thinking the more you'll get out
of what you see. For thinking is *digesting*. If I'm writing in a
preaching tone I'm just an ass! but the fact remains that if you're
bored a lot it means that your mental digestion isn't what it
should be. I think a good remedy for this is sometimes opening
your eyes wider. Sometimes a book helps a little, e.g. T's 'Hadshi
Murat' wouldn't be bad. If you can't get it in America let me
know. I *might* be able to get it here. [11]

In a subsequent letter he said of this book, which he sent to me, 'I
hope you'll get a lot out of it, because there is a lot *in* it.' Of its
author, Tolstoy, he remarked, 'There's a *real* man; who has a *right*
to write.' In reply to an observation of mine, he says in the same
letter, 'Yes, I think I understand why a ship isn't a good place for
"thinking"—I mean, *apart* from the fact you're very busy.' [13]

When Wittgenstein and I later talked about his own service in
the First World War he said emphatically that he had never been
bored, and I believe that he even said that he did not dislike his
army service. He related how he kept a notebook in his rucksack
and whenever he had a chance wrote in it the thoughts that com-
pose his first book, the *Tractatus Logico-Philosophicus*.

In the first letter that mentions *Hadji Murat*, there is a reference
to the state of preparation of Wittgenstein's new book, the *Philosophical Investigations*:

My work is going damn slowly. I wish I could get a volume
ready for publishing by next autumn; but I probably shan't. I'm a
bloody bad worker! [11]

Two months later (August 1945), he says:

I've been working a good deal this last academic year, I mean for
myself, & *if* everything goes well I might publish by Christmas.
Not that what I've produced is good, but it is now about as good
as I can make it. I think when it'll be finished I ought to come
into the open with it. [12]

But the next month:

> My work isn't going well; partly because I've contracted some trouble with one of my kidneys. Nothing serious, but it makes me jumpy & bad tempered. (I've always got some excuse). [14]

A fortnight later:

> my book is gradually nearing its final form, & if you're a good boy & come to Cambridge I'll let you read it. It'll probably disappoint you. And the truth is: its pretty lousy. (Not that I could improve on it essentially if I tried for another 100 years.) [15]

In this same letter he speaks of the possibility of resigning 'the absurd job of a prof. of philosophy' which, he says, 'is a kind of living death'. Four months later he says:

> My lectures begin in 3 days. I'll talk a lot of rubbish. It would be nice if you could come to Cambridge for an academic year before I resign my job! It might be a good thing, & a good conclusion for my dubious professorial career. [20]

I had read Tolstoy's novel *Resurrection* and was greatly impressed by the passage which opens chapter 59, beginning with the sentence: 'One of the most widespread superstitions is that every man has his own special definite qualities: that he is kind, cruel, wise, stupid, energetic, apathetic, and so on.' I had quoted the passage to Wittgenstein, which led him to make the following comment:

> I once tried to read 'Resurrection' but couldn't. You see, when Tolstoy just tells a story he impresses me infinitely more than when he addresses the reader. When he turns his back to the reader then he seems to me *most* impressive. Perhaps one day we can talk about this. It seems to me his philosophy is most true when it's *latent* in the story. [15]

In another letter he says:

> The other day I read Johnson's 'Life of Pope' & I liked it very much. As soon as I get to Cambridge I'm going to send you a little book 'Prayers & Meditations' by Johnson. You may not like it at all,—on the other hand you may. I do. [14]

He did send it to me, and said in an accompanying note:

> This is the little book I promised to send you. It seems to be out of print so I'm sending you my own copy. I wish to say that nor-

mally I can't read any printed prayers but that Johnson's
impressed me by being *human*. Perhaps you'll see what I mean if
you read them. As likely as not you won't like then *at all*.
Because you will probably not look at them from the *angle* from
which I see them. (But you might.) If you don't like the book
throw it away. Only first cut out the leaf with my dedication. For
when I shall become *very* famous it'll become very valuable as an
autograph, & your grandchildren may be able to sell it for a lot of
'dough'. [16]

In a letter from Wales he writes:

My landlord has a modern American translation of the Bible. I
dislike the translation of the N.T. (by a man E. J. Goodspeed) but
the translation of the O.T. (by a group of people) makes a lot of
things clearer to me & seems to me *well* worth reading. Perhaps
you'll see it one day. [15]

I had begun to read Freud, found him fascinating, and said something about this to Wittgenstein. He replied (December 1945):

I, too, was greatly impressed when I first read Freud. He's extraordinary.—Of course he is full of fishy thinking & his charm &
the charm of the subject is so great that you may easily be fooled.

He always stresses what great forces in the mind, what strong
prejudices work against the idea of psycho-analysis. But he never
says what an enormous charm that idea has for people, just as it
has for Freud himself. There may be strong prejudices against
uncovering something nasty, but sometimes it is infinitely more
attractive than it is repulsive. Unless you think *very* clearly
psycho-analysis is a dangerous & a foul practice, & it's done no
end of harm &, comparatively, very little good. (If you think I'm
an old spinster—think again!—All this, of course, doesn't detract
from Freud's extraordinary scientific achievement. Only, extraordinary scientific achievements have a way these days, of being
used for the destruction of human beings (I mean their bodies, or
their souls, *or their intelligence*). *So hold on to your brains.* [18]

In the spring of 1946, Wittgenstein wrote:

I feel *very* perturbed in my mind. I haven't done any decent work
for ages apart from my classes. They went all right last term. But
now my brain feels burnt out, as though only the four walls were
left standing, & some charred remains! Let's hope that I'll be in

moderately good condition when you'll be here! . . . Tomorrow's
my first lecture. *Oh hell!!* . . . I wish you a better head & a better
heart than I have. [21]

Our correspondence terminated because I arrived in Cambridge
with my family in the autumn of 1946 to stay for what turned out
to be the last year that Wittgenstein held his chair. Wittgenstein
came to our house on Searle Street, near Jesus Green, once or twice
a week. At first he was suspicious of my wife, whom he had not
previously met, as he was of all 'dons' wives', but soon he got over
this. When he came to supper he would sometimes insist on washing up the dishes. He had the idea that this could be done more effi-
ciently in the bath tub, where a continuous stream of hot water
was available from the geyser. More than once he washed the
dishes there, not dissuaded by the severity of the back-bending.
Wittgenstein had rigorous standards of cleanliness. He was dis-
turbed if he thought that we were washing up without an adequate
supply of soap or clean, hot water. He presented my wife with a
dish mop, as an improvement on a dishcloth.

Wittgenstein lectured for three terms that year on topics belonging to the philosophy of psychology. I took notes the first two or
three lectures but gave up this practice when I found that Wittgenstein was addressing a great many questions to me and that it was
impossible for me to say anything intelligent in reply if I was occupied with writing. (Peter Geach took notes of all the lectures,
which are preserved.) Wittgenstein said to me at the conclusion of
one of the first classes that he expected me to take an active part in
the discussions. I resolved to do my best, and throughout the year I
made a great effort to follow his thoughts during those meetings,
an exertion that left my mind utterly exhausted at the end of two
hours. The classes were even more exciting for me than they had
been seven years before. I understood Wittgenstein's ideas better,
although still not well, and the astonishing depth and originality of
his thinking was strikingly evident to me. Frequently after the lectures I wrote down brief résumés of what I had understood. I will
transcribe from my notes of a few lectures in order to give samples
of the sort of questions that Wittgenstein asked and the thoughts
that he produced in reply to them. These notes were not intended
to be verbatim, although sometimes they may have been partly so.
They were merely summaries of my recollections of the ideas that
impressed me most in each lecture. These summaries were not set

down until several hours after the lecture and frequently not until a day or two later.

In one lecture he talked about the notion of an *explanation* of the uses of an expression:

In supposing that the colour red (and also the phenomenon of thinking something to oneself) is something specific and indescribable, one supposes that one could learn what red is simply by seeing a red image. But what if I hit you on the head, and thereafter you were able to use the word 'red' correctly? Would this be an explanation of what red is? Of course not. An explanation is not *anything* that produces understanding. A key is not *anything* which opens a door.

A man might say: 'I know this book is red, because I have a mental impression of red.' But how does he know that he remembers the impression correctly? And how does he *compare* the impression with the book?

An explanation cannot be something private. It must be public. An explanation must provide a technique for getting somewhere. It must show the way. It must provide a method for using the word.

So if someone says 'I can show myself what thinking is, although I can't show anyone else,' we reply that he may do something which makes it possible for him to use the word correctly, but that this may not be at all what we call 'explaining' or 'showing'.

It may be objected to our method as follows: 'If someone asks what *time* is, you ask in return, "How do we measure time?" But time and the measurement of time are two different things. It is as if someone asked "What is a book?" and you replied, "How does one obtain a book?" '

This objection conceives that we know what *time* is, and we know what *measuring* is, *so* we know what measuring time is. But this is not true. If I have taught you to measure lengths, and then say, 'Now go ahead and measure time,' this will mean nothing.

Consider a tribe of people who measure lengths of fields by striding along and counting their steps. If different results are obtained for the same field, they think nothing of it!—even if payments depend on the results of the counting! If you come along and say that you have a better method which uses a tape measure, they might be quite uninterested. They might say: 'What a queer method that uses troublesome gadgets and always gets the same result! Our method is much better.'

The notion of a more accurate measurement does not enter into their lives, and so the notion of the *real* length does not either. If we say 'They *must* have the notion of a *real* length,' this is only because we imagine a more complicated life in which one method of measuring is preferred to another. But that is not their life.

Another time Wittgenstein discussed our knowledge of our bodily posture and the position of our limbs:

In order to move my arm voluntarily I must know what position it is in and whether I have moved it. Now how do I know what the position of my hand is, when I am not looking at it or feeling it with the other hand? How do I know, e.g., that my fingers are bent? There is a temptation to say 'I feel that they are bent.' This is a peculiar reply. For do you always have a certain feeling when your fingers are bent in that way; have you always noticed that feeling; and what feeling is it?

The feeling that my fingers are bent: is it subject to more and less, to *degrees*, as are feelings of temperature and pressure? No. This may show that 'I feel that my fingers are bent' means nothing different from 'I know that they are bent.' If we try to say what feelings of temperature, pressure, etc. go to make up this feeling that my fingers are bent, we shall see that it is not easy to say what they are, and furthermore we see that we rarely have them.

There *could* be cases in which I knew the position of my hand by a certain feeling. Also it may be true that if my hand were anaesthetized I should *not* know its position. But from this it does not follow that normally I know the position of my hand by certain sensations.

The question, 'How do I know my fingers are bent?' is just like the question, 'How do I know where my pain is?' I don't need to be shown where my pain is. My pointing gesture and verbal description *locates* the pain. Likewise I don't need to find out the posture of my body.

The notes from another meeting read as follows:

There is a philosophical question as to what one *really sees*.

Does one really see depth, or physical objects, or sadness, or a face, etc.? There is a temptation to say that all of this is 'interpretation', 'hypothesis', etc., and that what one *really* sees is a flat surface of coloured patches.

But if I am required to describe what I see, I do it with physical-object expressions: e.g. 'I see the top of a tan table; on it is an ink bottle towards the right end', etc. I would not be able to describe it by referring only to coloured patches.

It might be thought that although I cannot describe it in words, at least I could paint it. But the fact is that I can hardly paint at all unless I know what physical *objects* I am painting.

A criterion of whether a painting is a correct representation of what I saw is that I *say* it is. But some things might be changed in the painting and yet I should still say that it is exactly what I saw.

We have the idea of an *ideal* model or an *ideal* description of what one sees at any time. But no such ideal description exists. There are numerous sorts of things which we call 'descriptions' of what we see. They are all *rough*. And 'rough' here does *not* mean 'approximation'. We have the mistaken idea that there is a certain exact description of what one sees at any given moment.

In one lecture he made some general remarks about his philosophical procedure:

What I give is the morphology of the use of an expression. I show that it has kinds of uses of which you had not dreamed. In philosophy one feels *forced* to look at a concept in a certain way. What I do is to suggest, or even invent, other ways of looking at it. I suggest possibilities of which you had not previously thought. You thought that there was one possibility, or only two at most. But I made you think of others. Furthermore, I made you see that it was absurd to expect the concept to conform to those narrow possibilities. Thus your mental cramp is relieved, and you are free to look around the field of use of the expression and to describe the different kinds of uses of it.

In addition to attending Wittgenstein's lectures, I met with him privately one afternoon a week. Wittgenstein proposed that we should read his book together. He lent me a typescript copy of it. It was the writing that was posthumously published as Part I of the *Investigations*. Our procedure at the weekly meeting was the following: We sat in his living-room with our canvas chairs close together so that both of us could read the typescript. Starting at the beginning of the work, Wittgenstein first read a sentence aloud in German, then translated it into English, then made some remarks to me about the meaning of it. He then went to the next sentence; and so on. At the following meeting he started at the place where we had last stopped. At first I was flattered by this treatment. Wittgenstein once said to me, 'The reason I am doing this is so there will be at least one person who will understand my book when it is published.' After a time, however, I began to feel that this method was too confining. I wished to have discussions that would start from various philosophical questions that were currently puzzling to me. And, indeed, he gradually relaxed this procedure, and our discussions became more free.

Once when we were together he made a striking observation about philosophy: 'A person caught in a philosophical confusion is like a man in a room who wants to get out but doesn't know how. He tries the window but it is too high. He tries the chimney but it is too narrow. And if he would only *turn around*, he would see that the door has been open all the time!' This comment is related to remarks in *Investigations*, §§ 108, 123, 309. (Wittgenstein once observed in a lecture that there is a similarity between his conception of philosophy (e.g. 'the problems are solved, not by giving new information, but by arranging what we have always known', *Investigations*, § 109; 'the work of the philosopher consists in assembling reminders for a particular purpose', ibid., § 127) and the Socratic doctrine that knowledge is reminiscence: although he believed that there were also other things involved in the latter.)

After about two hours of reading or discussion, we would go for a walk and then have tea at Lyons, or in the restaurant above the Regal cinema. Sometimes he came to my house in Searle Street for supper. Once after supper, Wittgenstein, my wife, and I went for a walk on Midsummer Common. We talked about the movements of the bodies of the solar system. It occurred to Wittgenstein that the three of us should represent the movements of the sun, earth, and moon, relative to one another. My wife was the sun and maintained a steady pace across the meadow; I was the earth and circled her at a trot. Wittgenstein took the most strenuous part of all, the moon, and ran around me while I circled my wife. Wittgenstein entered into this game with great enthusiasm and seriousness, shouting instructions at us as he ran. He became quite breathless and dizzy with exhaustion.

Wittgenstein was fond of the fairs that came occasionally to Midsummer Common. He liked to roll pennies for prizes. He refused to try to direct the course of the penny, even closing his eyes before releasing it, because 'everything must be left to chance'. He was somewhat disapproving when my wife tried to direct the motion of her penny. He persuaded me to throw balls at targets, was excited while I did so, and afterwards extolled my modest prowess in extravagant terms.

Once when we were conversing Wittgenstein was delighted to learn that I knew Tolstoy's *Twenty-three Tales*. He had an extremely high opinion of these stories. He questioned me closely to find out whether I had understood the moral of the one entitled 'How Much Land Does A Man Need?' Wittgenstein had been stiff with me at the beginning of the conversation because he was displeased with me for a reason I have forgotten. But when he discovered that I had read, understood, and valued Tolstoy's stories, he became friendly and animated. Wittgenstein also admired the writings of Dostoevsky. He had read *The Brothers Karamazov* an extraordinary number of times; but he once said that *The House of the Dead* was Dostoevsky's greatest work.

Wittgenstein was persuaded to have weekly 'at-homes' during term-time that year. They were on Saturday afternoons from five to seven. Philosophical discussions occurred on questions raised by those attending. Although these meetings were less formal than his classes, in the sense that coming late was not an offence and consistent attendance was not required, nevertheless their atmosphere was serious to the point of solemnity. Normally about half a dozen people came. As we arrived one by one we found Wittgenstein sitting in silence in his canvas deck-chair, greeting no one, his face stern, apparently engrossed in serious reflection. No one dared to break the silence with an idle remark. We sat quietly as if absorbed in thought. Peter Geach once observed that it had the appearance of a Quaker prayer meeting. It took nerve to shatter this silence by introducing a topic. As soon as someone did, however, Wittgenstein was all attention—trying to grasp the meaning of the question, expanding or reformulating it, connecting it with other questions that at first seemed unrelated, and always, by his passionate intensity and force, endowing the question with dramatic interest. Topics in aesthetics were perhaps the most frequent at these at-homes, and the depth and richness of Wittgenstein's thinking about art were very exciting.

At one of the at-homes, Wittgenstein related a riddle for the purpose of throwing some light on the nature of philosophy. It went as follows: Suppose that a cord was stretched tightly around the earth at the equator. Now suppose that a piece one yard long was added to the cord. If the cord was kept taut and circular in form, how much above the surface of the earth would it be? Without stopping to work it out, everyone present was inclined to say that the distance of the cord from the surface of the earth would be so *minute* that it would be imperceptible. But this is wrong. The actual distance would be nearly six inches. Wittgenstein declared that this is the *kind* of mistake that occurs in philosophy. It consists in being *misled by a picture*. In the riddle the picture that misleads us is the comparison of the length of the additional piece with the length of the whole cord. The picture itself is correct enough: for a piece one yard long would be an insignificant fraction of the length of the whole cord. But we are misled by it to draw a wrong conclusion. A similar thing happens in philosophy: we are constantly deceived by mental pictures which are in themselves correct. Another striking illustration of a misleading picture that Wittgenstein gave, was a drawing of the earth as a ball with the people at the antipodes upside down and ourselves rightside up. The drawing, he said, does not misrepresent; yet it tempts us to think that the inhabitants of the antipodes are *beneath* us, and that they really hang head downwards. (This illustration is discussed in *Investigations*, § 351.)

Wittgenstein devoted a great deal of time to students that year. There were his two weekly classes of two hours each, his weekly at-home of two hours, a whole afternoon spent with me, another whole afternoon spent with Elizabeth Anscombe and W. A. Hijab, and finally the weekly evening meeting of the Moral Science Club which he usually attended. The atmosphere of the discussions at the latter was extremely disagreeable to Wittgenstein. He went only out of a sense of duty, thinking that he ought to do what he could to help make the discussions as decent as possible. After the paper was read, Wittgenstein was invariably the first one to speak, and he completely dominated the discussion as long as he was present. He believed, as he told me, that it was not good for the Club that he should always play such a prominent role there, but on the other hand it was quite impossible for him not to participate in the discussions with his characteristic force. His solution was to leave the meetings at the end of an hour and a half or two hours. The result was that the discussion was exciting and important while Wittgenstein was present, but trivial, flat, and anticlimactic after he left.

In all of these meetings—lectures, at-homes, private discussions and Club meetings—Wittgenstein gave his thoughts without stint. There was never any attempt by him to preserve his researches in secrecy. Furthermore, in every one of these discussions he was trying to *create*. The force of will and spirit that he exerted was awesome. As he struggled to work through a problem one frequently felt that one was in the presence of real suffering. Wittgenstein liked to draw an analogy between philosophical thinking and swimming: just as one's body has a natural tendency towards the surface and one has to make an *exertion* to get to the *bottom*—so it is with thinking. In talking about human greatness, he once remarked that he thought that the measure of a man's greatness would be in terms of what his work *cost* him. There is no doubt that Wittgenstein's philosophical labours cost him a great deal.

Wittgenstein had an extraordinary gift for divining the thoughts of the person with whom he was engaged in discussion. While the other struggled to put his thought into words Wittgenstein would perceive what it was and state it for him. This power of his, which sometimes seemed uncanny, was made possible, I am sure, by his own prolonged and continuous researches. He knew what someone else was thinking because he had *himself* travelled innumerable times through those twists and turns of reasoning. He once remarked to me that it was very unlikely that anyone in his classes should think of something of which he had not already thought. This was not braggadocio.

His heavy programme of that year put him under a great strain. He was sometimes troubled as to whether he should meet still other demands. For example, one man had come half-way around the world, at considerable sacrifice, in order to study with Wittgenstein. He wished to have private discussions with Wittgenstein, in addition to the lectures. Wittgenstein worried over this request. He felt under some obligation to meet it: on the other hand, he believed that he must conserve his strength. I think that he finally turned down the request. But it was typical of him to consider such a matter always in the light of what his *duty* was.

On the outskirts of Cambridge was a camp where German prisoners-of-war were confined. Wittgenstein had been a prisoner in the First War and was anxious to do something that might help to make the lives of these men more tolerable. He took me with him on a visit to the camp. He received permission to confer with a prisoners' representative. As a result of this conference I believe that Wittgenstein subsequently provided some musical instruments and music for the prisoners.

An incident occurred that winter which greatly excited and upset Wittgenstein. A certain philosopher published in a literary and critical journal an article that purported to give a popular account of contemporary British philosophy. Of Wittgenstein the article said that the nature of his philosophical work since the publication of the *Tractatus* was unknown; but that if one were to judge from the writings of a leading disciple, philosophy, in Wittgenstein's hands, had become a kind of psychoanalysis. Someone showed this article to Wittgenstein and he was extremely angered by it. He said that the author merely pretended to be ignorant of his work. What made Wittgenstein furious was not only his belief in the author's dishonesty, but also the implication that Wittgenstein kept the nature of his work a secret. He said that he had always regarded his lectures as a form of publication. (I should mention here that two volumes of material which he had dictated to students, known as 'The Blue Book' and 'The Brown Book', had been circulating privately, in mimeograph or typescript form, for more than ten years and had been widely read by British philosophers.) I believe another thing that angered him was the suggestion that in his conception philosophy was a form of psychoanalysis, a suggestion that I had heard him explicitly attack, on two occasions, as based on a confusion. 'They are different techniques', he had said.

This article threw Wittgenstein into a great state for several days. He asked me whether I would publish a reply to it. My answer was that I did not have the least idea what form a reply could take. Wittgenstein disliked this answer. He wanted to know whether I would undertake to defend Moore, in print, if someone were to say false and unjust things about *his* philosophical work. I felt compelled to say that I would. Wittgenstein then exclaimed that this confirmed what he had always suspected—namely, that his friends regarded *him* as 'Vogelfrei': that is, as an outlaw, a bird at whom anyone had a right to shoot. I believe that Wittgenstein asked both Anscombe and Smythies whether they would publish a reply to the article, but did not get an affirmative answer. To the former he repeated the expression 'Vogelfrei'. For two or three days Wittgenstein was in a real frenzy about the matter. He even contemplated sending a reply of his own to the same journal. Also he talked seriously of taking his typescript (Part I of the *Investigations*) to the Cambridge University Press for immediate publication. After a few days he calmed down. He said that he was not going to be 'stampeded' into publishing prematurely. He did write a private note to the author of the article, in which he said that he believed that the latter had more knowledge of the nature of Wittgenstein's philosophical researches than he had represented in the article. Wittgenstein received a polite and deferential note in reply, and the incident was closed.

Wittgenstein expressed more than once the fear that his writings would be destroyed by fire. He related with horror how the great historian, Mommsen, had lost a manuscript volume of his History of Rome in that way. Wittgenstein purchased a light steel safe in which he kept his notebooks and manuscripts in his living-room at Trinity. He said more than once that though he doubted that he would publish any of this work in his lifetime he definitely wished to have his book (Part I of the *Investigations*) published after his death. On the other hand, he once exclaimed to me with vehemence that he would gladly see all of his writings destroyed if along with them would vanish the publications of his pupils and disciples. He was sometimes visited by the fear that when his work was finally published posthumously the learned world might believe that he had obtained his ideas from philosophers whom he had taught, because there might be some resemblances between his work and those writings of theirs that had been published before his own. He asked me very earnestly if I would defend him, after his death, from any such claim or rumour that might arise, and I told him that I would. His anxiety on this matter is reflected in the preface of the *Investigations*: 'For more than one reason what I publish here will have points of contact with what other people are writing today.—If my remarks do not bear a stamp which marks them as mine,—I do not wish to lay any further claim to them as my property.'

Wittgenstein had strong feelings about plagiarism. He gave me an account of his relationship with a certain man, about which there had been many rumours. Wittgenstein said that Moritz Schlick, this man, and himself had met together for some philosophical discussions, and that he had set forth some of his ideas while they took notes. Sometime later he had seen a paper of this man's which had been accepted for publication and which was not only based on Wittgenstein's ideas but even used Wittgenstein's own illustrations. This article did contain an acknowledgement but phrased in such a manner as to suggest that while the author had derived a certain amount of stimulation from talks with Wittgenstein the main work was, of course, his own. Wittgenstein was extremely incensed. He said that he took the matter up with Schlick, who was 'a decent human being', and that the latter promised to do something about it. But there occurred just then the sudden death of Schlick by assassination, and so the paper was published without adequate acknowledgement of indebtedness.

Wittgenstein was almost as much angered by imperfect representations of his thoughts as by the plagiarism of them. He told me of an incident involving a young lady who had attended his lectures. She wrote an article which was intended to present Wittgenstein's views on a certain topic. She submitted it to Moore, the editor of *Mind*, and also showed it to Wittgenstein. Wittgenstein thought it was very bad and told her that she *could not* publish it. When she persisted in her intention to publish, Wittgenstein went to Moore to persuade him not to print it. He said to Moore: 'You attended those lectures. You know that her account of them is bad!' According to Wittgenstein, Moore admitted that 'It wasn't good', but was not dissuaded from publishing the piece. It was clear to me that Wittgenstein had been very much vexed and excited by this incident. Probably it is one of the things to which he refers in the preface of the *Investigations*: ' . . . I was obliged to learn that my results (which I had communicated in lectures, typescripts and discussions), variously misunderstood, more or less mangled or watered down, were in circulation. This stung my vanity and I had difficulty in quieting it.'

Although considerations of reputation were certainly not unknown to his nature, and could even become violent, as in the episodes just related, it must be remembered, on the other hand, that Wittgenstein purposely lived in obscurity, discouraging all attempts to make him into a celebrity or public figure, which otherwise he would certainly have become.

His conception of the value of his own work would not be easy to describe. In the preface of the *Investigations* he says that it is not 'a good book', and this remark was not an affectation of modesty. He certainly believed that the work might have been made better, although not by himself. To Dr. Louise Mooney, who treated him when he was ill in the summer of 1949, and to whom he talked a little about his work, he exclaimed: 'Maybe it is all mistaken; maybe it is all wrong.' But this was not a characteristic attitude. He expounded and defended his ideas in argument with confidence and power. He did not think of the central conceptions of his philosophy as *possibly* in error. He certainly believed most of the time, that he had produced an important advance in philosophy. Yet I think that he was inclined to feel that the importance of this advance might be exaggerated by those who were too close to it. This feeling is probably reflected in his choice of Nestroy's remark for the motto of the *Investigations*: 'Überhaupt hat der Fortschritt das an sich, dass er viel grösser ausschaut, als er wirklich ist.' (It is the nature of every advance, that it appears much greater than it actually is.)

With regard to the question of what the future would hold for his work—whether it would disappear without leaving a mark, or whether, if it continued to live, it would prove any help to mankind—he was in doubt. Freud once remarked in a letter: 'As to the question of the value of my work and its influence on the future development of science I myself find it very hard to form an opinion. Sometimes I believe in it; sometimes I doubt. I don't think there is any way of predicting it; perhaps God himself doesn't yet know.'[2] I think that these sentences would also serve very well to express Wittgenstein's attitude towards his own work, with the exception that his inclination to pessimism was stronger than Freud's. I do not believe that Wittgenstein ever thought of his work as *great*.

Wittgenstein sometimes doubted his friends, as illustrated by the 'Vogelfrei' incident. He suspected that they were not attached to him by affection but rather by their interest in him as a source of philosophical inspiration. He once told me that he had given away his fortune, when a young man, so that he would not have any friends on account of it, but now he feared that he had friends for the sake of the philosophy they could get out of him. He wanted friends who were not trying to *get anything* out of him. Another time he said: 'Although I cannot *give* affection, I have a great *need* for it.' Human kindness, human concern, was for him a far more

[2] Ernest Jones, *Sigmund Freud* (London, 1955), vol. ii, p. 446.

important attribute in a person than intellectual power or culti-
vated taste. He related with pleasure an incident that happened to
him in Wales. He had taken lodgings in the home of a preacher.
The first time that Wittgenstein presented himself at this house
the lady of the house had inquired of Wittgenstein whether he
would like some tea, and whether he would also like this and that
other thing. Her husband called to her from another room: 'Do not
ask; *give!*' Wittgenstein was most favourably impressed by this
exclamation. A characteristic remark that Wittgenstein would
make when referring to someone who was notably generous or
kind or honest was 'He is a *human being!*'—thus implying that
most people fail even to be human.

Undoubtedly Wittgenstein did greatly need human warmth and
affection and he was enormously appreciative of any simple kindness. But a friendly relationship with him was very exacting. He
could rebuke a friend with extreme harshness. He had a tendency
to be suspicious of motives and character. Sometimes his judgements were precipitous and in error. But on the whole he formed
acute and realistic estimates of his friends. As Smythies remarked,
when Wittgenstein gave one a lashing one usually had it coming.
One learned things about oneself from Wittgenstein's rebukes. He
was particularly hard on all forms of vanity, affectation, or com-
placency.

But Wittgenstein could be excessively severe with a friend, as
some of the previous incidents may have shown. Another illustration, perhaps amusing, is the following: In his rooms at Trinity
he kept a small potted flowering plant. When he left Cambridge
between terms to go to Wales, he left this plant at our house. I am
afraid that we were negligent, sometimes leaving the plant too near
an electric heater. It began to look sickly and the leaves and buds
gradually dropped off. When Wittgenstein came back to Cambridge
I returned the plant to his rooms, although it was then quite dead.
A few days later he and my wife had a chance meeting in the street,
the first since his departure for Wales six weeks previously. Without any greeting he said severely: 'I see that you know nothing
about plants!' and walked off without another word. My wife was
upset. When he next came to our house no further mention of the
plant was made.

It was always a strain to be with Wittgenstein. Not only were the
intellectual demands of his conversation very great, but there was
also his severity, his ruthless judgements, his tendency to be cen-

sorious, and his depression. Each time that I spent several hours with him in the winter of 1946–7 my mind would be exhausted and my nerves frayed. My typical feeling was that I could not bear to see him again for some days.

Several times that winter Wittgenstein expressed a doubt that he would continue to serve in his chair. Undoubtedly the idea of being a *professional* philosopher was very repugnant to him. Universities and academic life he disliked intensely. He was exhausted by his strenuous programme of lectures and discussions. Perhaps more importantly, he believed that his influence as a teacher was largely harmful. He was disgusted and pained by what he observed of the half-understanding of his philosophical ideas, or a tendency towards a shallow cleverness in his students. He felt himself to be a failure as a teacher. This, I believe, was a source of constant torment to him. In his lectures he would sometimes exclaim in a tone of real suffering: 'I am a dreadful teacher!' He once concluded a year's lectures with this sentence: 'The only seed that I am likely to sow is a certain jargon.'

Apart from other things, I think that there was indeed something in the content of his philosophy that, improperly assimilated, had and still has an unfortunate effect on those influenced by it. I refer to his conception that words are not used with 'fixed' meanings (*Investigations*, § 79), that concepts do not have 'sharp boundaries' (ibid., §§ 68, 76). This teaching, I believe, produced a tendency in his students to assume that precision and thoroughness were not required in their own thinking. From this tendency nothing but slovenly philosophical work could result.

The considerations in favour of resigning his chair were acquiring more and more force in Wittgenstein's mind. This was particularly revealed by an incident involving a certain philosopher, with whom I was acquainted. The latter wrote to me in the winter of 1946–7 that he wished to spend the next year in Cambridge and wondered whether he could obtain permission to attend Wittgenstein's lectures. I took the matter up with Wittgenstein. As I recall, he wrote directly to this man, giving him permission. But Wittgenstein asked me to write to him too and caution him that it was not impossible that he would resign his chair before the next academic year. Wittgenstein wished me, rather than himself, to convey this warning, in order not to give rise to rumour. I did as he wished. Then in the summer of 1947 he did go to see the Vice-Chancellor in order to submit his resignation. But there he was informed that he was entitled to a term of sabbatical leave; and he was persuaded to take leave during the Michaelmas term of 1947 and to postpone the question of his resignation. He then asked me to inform the above man of the change in his plans, and to say that so far as was then known Wittgenstein would lecture during the Lent term, although the possibility that he would resign still existed. I did as requested. When in the autumn Wittgenstein did resign his chair, the man in question was greatly incensed and made (as will be seen) absurd and unjust accusations against Wittgenstein, as if under the impression that the latter had deliberately misled him, or as if Wittgenstein was under an obligation to remain in his chair because this man had expected to attend his lectures. The fact is that Wittgenstein had shown unusual consideration.

Wittgenstein was widely regarded by people who did not know him as a mysterious and eccentric figure. He was the object not only of hostility but also of innumerable fantastic rumours. Once in Cambridge I heard one undergraduate in earnestness inform another that Wittgenstein delivered his lectures while lying on the floor and gazing at the ceiling. When he was living in my house in the States it was reported that his residence was a barn and that I was the only person who could have access to him. And later when he was living in a cottage on the Irish coast I heard a grave rumour that he was herding goats in Turkey.

An undergraduate who lived a floor or two below Wittgenstein's rooms in Whewell's Court kept a piano on which he frequently practised. The sounds penetrated to Wittgenstein's rooms and almost drove him mad, especially when the music was familiar to him. It was impossible for him to think when he heard the piano. He solved this problem in a characteristic way. He obtained a large, second-hand electric fan which produced a uniform noise in sufficient volume to drown the piano. I was in his rooms for discussions several times when the fan was going, but found the roar of it completely distracting, whereas Wittgenstein was not bothered in the least.

The mathematical physicist, Freeman Dyson, then an undergraduate, lived in the set of rooms adjacent to Wittgenstein's. Once Wittgenstein invited him to tea. The conversation, as Dyson told me, was first about the nature of Dyson's studies. Then the latter, out of politeness, asked Wittgenstein what the nature of his own work was. Wittgenstein was at first wary, wanting to know whether Dyson was a 'journalist'. Assured that he was not, Wittgenstein then did talk to Dyson about the nature of philosophy and his own part in it. Dyson recalled one anecdote of Wittgenstein's which is of considerable interest: One day when Wittgenstein was passing a field where a football game was in progress the thought first struck him that in language we play *games* with *words*. A central idea of his philosophy, the notion of a 'language-game', apparently had its genesis in this incident. Dyson also recalled his last encounter with Wittgenstein. It was the end of the May term of 1946–7 and Dyson was packing his trunk at the bottom of the stairs in Whewell's Court. Wittgenstein, whom he had not seen for several weeks, came down the stairs with his walking stick, raincoat and tweed cap. He nodded to Dyson and started to walk past, but then stopped and said: 'My mind is getting stupider and stupider!' He then walked off without another word.

What the relationship of Wittgenstein was to the famous 'verification principle' ('The meaning of a statement is its method of verification') of Logical Positivism has often been a subject of curiosity. Wittgenstein told me an anecdote that sheds some light on this. The philosopher and psychologist, G. F. Stout, came to Cambridge for a brief visit and Wittgenstein invited him to tea. (My impression is that this was in the early 30s.) Stout said to Wittgenstein that he had heard that Wittgenstein had something interesting and important to say about *verification*, and that he would like very much to know about it. Both of them knew that Stout had to leave very shortly to catch a train and Wittgenstein would not ordinarily, as he told me, have tried to make any kind of philosophical remark in such circumstances. But Stout's seriousness and genuine desire to understand Wittgenstein's teaching on this point so impressed him that he related to Stout the following parable: Imagine that there is a town in which the policemen are required to obtain information from each inhabitant, e.g. his age, where he came from, and what work he does. A record is kept of this information and some use is made of it. Occasionally when a policeman questions an inhabitant he discovers that the latter does not do *any* work. The policeman enters this fact on the record, because *this too* is a useful piece of information about the man!

The application of the parable is, I think, that if you do not understand a statement, then to discover that it has no verification is an important piece of information about it and makes you understand it better. That is to say, you understand it *better*; you do not find out that there is nothing to understand.

During his final year as a professor Wittgenstein used to visit Moore about once every fortnight. Wittgenstein respected Moore's honesty and seriousness, and once he said that Moore was 'deep'. At the same time talks with Moore almost always depressed him, because Moore was so 'childlike'. Wittgenstein once remarked that what Moore primarily did, as a philosopher, was to 'destroy premature solutions' of philosophical problems, which struck me as an acute characterization. But he added that he did not believe that Moore would *recognize* a *correct* solution if he were presented with one. He said that he had attended Moore's lectures only a few times, when he was a student at Cambridge before World War I, because he could not bear the repetitiousness that always characterized them. He once remarked that the only work of Moore's that greatly impressed him was his discovery of the peculiar kind of nonsense involved in such a sentence as 'It is raining but I don't believe it.' (This is referred to as 'Moore's paradox' in *Investigations*, Part II, sect. x.) But he admitted that Moore's 'defence of common sense' was an important idea. He observed that if one were trying to find exactly the right words to express a fine distinction of thought, Moore was absolutely the best person to consult.

Wittgenstein related to me an anecdote about Moore that, he thought, exhibited what was most admirable in Moore's character: Moore had been working hard on his lecture entitled 'Proof of an External World', which he was to deliver before the British Academy in London. He was very dissatisfied with the concluding part of it, but he had not been able to revise it in any way that satisfied him. On the day of the lecture, as he got ready to leave his house in Cambridge to catch the London train, Mrs. Moore said to him, 'Don't worry; I'm sure they'll like it.' To which Moore replied: 'If they *do* they'll be *wrong*!' I believe that this incident reveals that in Moore which Wittgenstein regarded as 'deep'.

Moore's health was quite good in 1946-7, but before that he had suffered a stroke and his doctor had advised that he should not become greatly excited or fatigued. Mrs. Moore enforced this prescription by not allowing Moore to have a philosophical discussion with anyone for longer than one hour and a half. Wittgenstein was extremely vexed by this regulation. He believed that Moore should not be supervised by his wife. He should discuss as long as he liked. If he became very excited or tired and had a stroke and died—well, that would be a decent way to die: with his boots on. Wittgenstein felt that it was unseemly that Moore, with his great love for truth, should be forced to break off a discussion before it had reached its proper end. I think that Wittgenstein's reaction to this regulation was very characteristic of his outlook on life. A human being should do the thing for which he has a talent with all of his energy his life long, and should never relax this devotion to his job merely in order to prolong his existence. This platonistic attitude was manifested again two years later when Wittgenstein, feeling that he was losing his own talent, questioned whether he should continue to live.

Wittgenstein more than once expressed admiration of the keenness of Bertrand Russell's intellect when the two of them worked together on problems of logic before the First World War. Russell was extremely 'bright', is how he put it: Moore, in comparison, was less so. Wittgenstein recalled with pleasure that one day, when Russell and himself had finished several hours of hard work together, Russell had exclaimed, 'Logic is *hell*!' This exclamation characterized Wittgenstein's attitude towards his own philosophical labours. Wittgenstein believed that the Theory of Descriptions was Russell's most important production, and he once remarked that it must have been an enormously difficult undertaking for him. But in 1946 Wittgenstein had a poor opinion of Russell's contemporary philosophical writings. 'Russell isn't going to kill himself doing philosophy now', he said with a smile. I noticed that on the infrequent occasions when both Russell and Wittgenstein were at the Moral Science Club, Wittgenstein was deferential to Russell in the discussion as I never knew him to be with anyone else.

Wittgenstein related to me two anecdotes pertaining to the *Tractatus*, which perhaps I should record, although he also told them to several other persons. One has to do with the origination of the central idea of the *Tractatus*—that a proposition is a *picture*. This idea came to Wittgenstein when he was serving in the Austrian army in the First War. He saw a newspaper that described the occurrence and location of an automobile accident by means of a diagram or map. It occurred to Wittgenstein that this map was a proposition and that therein was revealed the essential nature of propositions—namely, to *picture* reality.

The other incident has to do with something that precipitated the destruction of this conception. Wittgenstein and P. Sraffa, a lecturer in economics at Cambridge, argued together a great deal over the ideas of the *Tractatus*. One day (they were riding, I think, on a train) when Wittgenstein was insisting that a proposition and that which it describes must have the same 'logical form', the same 'logical multiplicity', Sraffa made a gesture, familiar to Neapolitans as meaning something like disgust or contempt, of brushing the underneath of his chin with an outward sweep of the finger-tips of one hand. And he asked: 'What is the logical form of *that*?' Sraffa's example produced in Wittgenstein the feeling that there was an absurdity in the insistence that a proposition and what it describes must have the same 'form'. This broke the hold on him of the conception that a proposition must literally be a 'picture' of the reality it describes.[3]

Wittgenstein frequently said to me disparaging things about the *Tractatus*. I am sure, however, that he still regarded it as an important work. For one thing, he was greatly concerned in the *Investigations* to refute the errors of the former book. Also he told me once that he really thought that in the *Tractatus* he had provided a perfected account of a view that is the *only* alternative to the viewpoint of his later work. For another thing, he definitely wanted the *Tractatus* to be republished jointly with his newer writings. As he says in the preface of the *Investigations*, it 'seemed to me that I should publish those old thoughts and the new ones together: that the latter could be seen in the right light only by contrast with and against the background of my old ways of thinking.'

At this point I should like to say what I can on the difficult subject of Wittgenstein's attitude towards religion. He told me that in his youth he had been contemptuous of it, but that at about the age of twenty-one something had caused a change in him. In Vienna he saw a play that was mediocre drama, but in it one of the characters expressed the thought that no matter what happened in the world, nothing bad could happen to *him*—he was independent of fate and circumstances. Wittgenstein was struck by this stoic thought; for the first time he saw the possibility of religion. He said that during his service in the First War he came across Tolstoy's writings on the Gospels, which made a great impression on him.

Wittgenstein says in the *Tractatus*: 'Not *how* the world is, is the mystical, but *that* it is' (§ 6.44). I believe that a certain feeling of

[3] Professor G. H. von Wright informs me that Wittgenstein related this incident to him somewhat differently: the question at issue, according to Wittgenstein, was whether every proposition must have a 'grammar', and Sraffa asked Wittgenstein what the 'grammar' of that gesture was. In describing the incident to von Wright, Wittgenstein did not mention the phrases 'logical form' or 'logical multiplicity'.

amazement that *anything should exist at all*, was sometimes experienced by Wittgenstein, not only during the *Tractatus* period, but also when I knew him.[4] Whether this feeling has anything to do with religion is not clear to me. But Wittgenstein did once say that he thought that he could understand the conception of God, in so far as it is involved in one's awareness of one's own sin and guilt. He added that he could *not* understand the conception of a *Creator*. I think that the ideas of Divine judgement, forgiveness, and redemption had some intelligibility for him, as being related in his mind to feelings of disgust with himself, an intense desire for purity, and a sense of the helplessness of human beings to make themselves better. But the notion of a being *making the world* had no intelligibility for him at all.

Wittgenstein once suggested that a way in which the notion of immortality can acquire a meaning is through one's feeling that one has duties from which one cannot be released, even by death. Wittgenstein himself possessed a stern sense of duty.

I believe that Wittgenstein was prepared by his own character and experience to comprehend the idea of a judging and redeeming God. But any cosmological conception of a Deity, derived from the notions of cause or of infinity, would be repugnant to him. He was impatient with 'proofs' of the existence of God, and with attempts to give religion a *rational* foundation. When I once quoted to him a remark of Kierkegaard's to this effect: 'How can it be that Christ does not exist, since I know that He has saved me?', Wittgenstein exclaimed: 'You see! It isn't a question of *proving* anything!' He disliked the theological writings of Cardinal Newman, which he read with care during his last year at Cambridge. On the other hand, he revered the writings of St. Augustine. He told me he decided to begin his *Investigations* with a quotation from the latter's *Confessions*, not because he could not find the conception

---

[4] After writing this sentence I learned that Wittgenstein once read a paper on Ethics (at a date not known to me, but probably soon after his return to Cambridge in 1929) in which he said that he sometimes had a certain experience which could best be described by saying that 'when I have it *I wonder at the existence of the world*. And I am then inclined to use such phrases as "How extraordinary that anything should exist!" or "How extraordinary that the world should exist!" He went on to say something that is related to the thought expressed in the above-mentioned play: namely, that he sometimes also had 'the experience of feeling *absolutely* safe. I mean the state of mind in which one is inclined to say "I am safe, nothing can injure me *whatever* happens."'

expressed in that quotation stated as well by other philosophers, but because the conception *must* be important if so great a mind held it. Kierkegaard he also esteemed. He referred to him, with something of awe in his expression, as a 'really religious' man. He had read the *Concluding Unscientific Postscript*—but found it 'too deep' for him. The *Journal* of George Fox, the English Quaker, he read with admiration—and presented me with a copy of it. He praised one of Dickens' sketches—an account of the latter's visit on board a passenger ship crowded with English converts to Mormonism, about to sail for America. Wittgenstein was impressed by the calm resolution of those people, as portrayed by Dickens.

I do not wish to give the impression that Wittgenstein accepted any religious faith—he certainly did not—or that he was a religious person.[5] But I think that there was in him, in some sense, the *possibility* of religion. I believe that he looked on religion as a 'form of life' (to use an expression from the *Investigations*) in which he did not participate, but with which he was sympathetic and which greatly interested him. Those who did participate he respected—although here as elsewhere he had contempt for insincerity. I suspect that he regarded religious belief as based on qualities of character and will that he himself did not possess. Of Smythies and Anscombe, both of whom had become Roman Catholics, he once said to me: 'I could not possibly bring myself to believe all the things that they believe.' I think that in this remark he was not disparaging their belief. It was rather an observation about his own capacity.

It was Wittgenstein's character to be deeply pessimistic, both about his own prospects and those of humanity in general. Anyone who was on an intimate footing with Wittgenstein must have been aware of the feeling in him that our lives are ugly and our minds in the dark—a feeling that was often close to despair.

In the summer of 1947 I left Cambridge with my family to return to the States. From America I wrote to Wittgenstein, thanking him for the thoughts that he had so generously imparted to me. He replied:

You know how much I enjoyed being with you at Cambridge. And, of course, you owe me *nothing*. My mind is rather in a turmoil these days. I am almost certain that I shall resign my professorship in the autumn . . . *please keep it to yourself* as it's not

---

[5] See Additional Note 1 on p. 82.

yet certain. I *hate* to let down Rollins & —— [*here he mentions the name of the man who wished to attend his lectures and whom I had warned, at Wittgenstein's request, of the possibility of his resignation*], but I think I won't be able to help it. I'ld like to be alone somewhere & try to write & to make at least one part of my book publishable. I'll never be able to do it while I'm teaching at Cambridge. Also I think that, quite apart from writing, I need a longish spell of thinking *alone*, without having to talk to anybody. But I haven't yet told the authorities about my plan & I don't intend to do so until October when I'll decide definitely. [22]

Three months later (November 1947), after a trip to Austria, he wrote:

As soon as I returned here from Austria I tendered my resignation to the Vice Chancellor & I shall cease to be professor on Dec. 31st. at 12 p.m. *Whatever* happens to me (& I'm not at all sanguine about my future) I feel I did the only natural thing.

This letter contained the following postscript:

I had an impertinent letter from [*here again occurs the name of the man to whom I had written at Wittgenstein's request*] reproaching me for not letting him know beforehand about my resignation. He told me that this showed a 'shocking' 'fault of character' & that I was 'a gross person'. I replied & tried to tell him 'where he gets off'. He *seems* to be an ass. [23]

In December Wittgenstein wrote from Red Cross, Wicklow, Eire:

I have only today moved into the above address. It's a little Guest House $2\frac{1}{2}$ to 3 hours by bus from Dublin. It's not *too* bad & I hope I'll acclimatize. I'm the only guest. Of course, right now I still feel completely strange & uncomfortable. . . . That I haven't worked a stroke for ages goes without saying . . . I wish you lots of luck & I know you wish me the same. Both of us need it like hell. And other people do too. [24]

A month later he wrote to my wife:

This is a pretty quiet place, & if it were still more quiet it would suit me *still* better. My work's going moderately well & I think it might even go very well if I weren't suffering from some kind of indigestion which I don't seem to be able to shake off. I'll have to come to Ithaca & eat your good cooking.

In response to her question as to the wisdom of requiring our eleven-year-old son to sometimes read aloud to us, he added:

> I think it's a *very* good idea to make Ray read to you. To practice reading aloud *well*, i.e. carefully, teaches one a *lot*! E.g. how rotten & slapdash most people, & the newspapers, write; & they write as they *think*. [25]

In February 1948 he wrote to me:

> I am now in very good bodily health & my work isn't going bad either. I have occasionally queer states of nervous instability about which I'll only say that they're rotten while they last, & teach one to pray.

I had previously written to him about two books—one was Kierkegaard's *The Works of Love*, which greatly impressed me, and the other was Prescott's *Conquest of Mexico*, which I had enjoyed. His letter continues:

> I've never read 'The works of love'. Kierkegaard is far too deep for me, anyhow. He bewilders me without working the good effects which he would in *deeper* souls.—Years ago Drury read to Skinner & me the beginning of the 'Conquest of Mexico' which we found very interesting indeed. That I didn't like the parsonish point of view of Prescott's is, of course, a different story.

He adds as a postscript:

> I haven't anyone at all to talk to here, & this is good & in a way bad. It would be good to see someone occasionally to whom one could say a really friendly word. I don't need *conversations*. What I'd like would be someone to smile at occasionally. [26]

Later he wrote from a new address, Rosro Cottage, Renvyle P.O., Co. Galway, Eire:

> I've had a bad time lately: soul, mind & body. I felt exceedingly depressed for many weeks, then fell ill & now I'm weak & completely dull. I haven't done any work for 5–6 weeks. I'm living alone in a cottage here on the west coast right on the sea, far from civilization. [28]

A month later (June 1948) he was in better spirits:

> Thanks a lot for the detective mags. I had, before they arrived, been reading a detective story by Dorothy Sayers, & it was so

bl. . . foul that it depressed me. Then when I opened one of your mags it was like getting out of a stuffy room into the fresh air. [29]

The next day, having discovered in one of the detective 'mags' a letter from my wife pressing him to visit us in the States, he replied to her as follows:

Thanks *a lot* for inviting me. It's good to know that you won't mind taking me in once the time is ripe. But it isn't now. You see, my main source of trouble is myself &, unfortunately, that would accompany me wherever I go. I'm *much* better now than before I came here. My health is as fine as can be expected of an old codger, & the things that I'm always inclined to beef about are *necessary* evils. My work, e.g., is only so-so; but then my talent is only *that* size & I'm getting a bit shop worn & nothing can help this. I often get exasperated about it but I just must (or *ought* to) learn to bear it. The solitude here is often a strain, but it's also a blessing; that I have to do all my housework is a great strain, but it's undoubtedly a great blessing, too, because it keeps me sane, it *forces* me to live a regular life & is in general good for me *although I curse it every day*. The truth is I oughtn't to be such an old woman & complain such a lot; but then that's also one of the things that can't be changed.—But I hope, *seriously*, to come & stay with you one day when I'll be riper for it. [30]

Still at Rosro Cottage in July, he writes to me:

My work isn't going well though it's moving a bit. The other day I asked myself: ought I to have left the University, oughtn't I to have gone on teaching after all? I immediately felt that I couldn't possibly have continued teaching philosophy & even told myself that perhaps I ought to have resigned sooner; but then I thought of you & v. Wright in Cambridge & said to myself that I'd left exactly at the right moment. If my philosophical talent comes to an end now it's bad luck, but that's all. [32]

He announced his intention of remaining at Rosro Cottage for another month and then going to Austria for three or four weeks. Apparently he did go to Austria, and after that spent a fortnight in Cambridge, in October 1948, dictating from his manuscripts. His next letter was written from Ross's Hotel, Parkgate Street, Dublin, in November. He had intended to stop there for only a short time to visit his friend, Drury, and then return to Rosro. But his plans changed:

> When I came here I found to my surprise that I could work again; & as I'm anxious to make hay during the very short period when the sun shines in my brain I've decided not to go to Rosro this winter but to stay here where I've got a warm & quiet room.

When I was in Cambridge in 1946–7 Wittgenstein had loaned me a typescript of the work that was later published as Part I of the *Investigations*, and which I had returned to him before departing for the States. I had just written to ask him whether he could send me a copy of it. To this he replied in the same letter:

> I should *like* you to have a typescript of my stuff but I don't see how I can let you have one at present. There exist only 3 copies. One I have (& I need it), Miss Anscombe has one, Moore has half, or $\frac{3}{4}$ of one & the remaining half or $\frac{1}{4}$ is somewhere among my things in Cambridge. There is no one here who could make another copy from mine, & it would cost a *lot* of money. Of course Miss Anscombe could send you her copy, but, to be quite honest, I'd rather it remained safely in England as long as there are only 3 copies existing. I hope you don't think me beastly. It's nice of you to want a copy of my stuff at all! I'll let you have one as soon as I can get another one made. [33]

As it turned out, when Wittgenstein came to visit us in America he brought the copy that Moore had had, and left it with me upon his return to England. After his death I put it in the hands of his literary executors.

My wife and I occasionally sent small parcels of foodstuffs to Wittgenstein, for which he was always extravagantly grateful. The following is a sample from a letter to my wife:

> Thank you & Norman ever so much for your wonderful present!

> As I've said before, you should be put under tutilage. And in that case I might try to get 'powers of attorney'. (That's the sort of thing I always read in my detective magazines.) Everything in the box was most useful & grand.

He was still at Ross's Hotel in Dublin, 'working a fair amount & still moderately well. I wish my luck could hold for another 6 months, for by then I could get a good chunk of work done.' [34]

Four weeks later (January 1949) he reports that his luck did not hold:

> I had a pretty good run of work in the last 3 months, or so, but I fell ill with some sort of infection of the intestines about 3 weeks ago & it hasn't yet cleared up. If it goes on for another week I shall consult a specialist. Of course it hasn't done my work any good. I had to interrupt it completely for a week & after that it just crawled along, as I do when I take a walk these days. [35]

A letter of mine to Wittgenstein at this time contained some comments about Moore. I wrote of how I had once told Moore that a well-known philosopher of my acquaintance tended to react with hostility to criticisms of his published philosophical views. Moore seeming to be surprised at this information, I asked him whether he could not understand how professional vanity might make a man resentful of criticism of his writings. Moore, to my astonishment, said 'No!' In relating this to Wittgenstein, I added that this ignorance of human nature was to Moore's credit. Wittgenstein replied:

> Now as to Moore:—I don't really understand Moore, &, therefore, what I'll say may be quite wrong. But this is what I'm inclined to say:—That Moore is in some sense extraordinarily childlike is obvious, & the remark you quoted (about vanity) is certainly an example of that childlikeness. There is also a *certain* innocence about Moore; he is, e.g., completely unvain. As to it's being to his *'credit'* to be childlike,—I can't understand that; unless it's also to a *child's* credit. For you aren't talking of the innocence a man has fought for, but of an innocence which comes from a natural absence of a temptation.—I believe that all you wanted to say was that you *liked*, or even *loved*, Moore's childlikeness. And that I can *understand*.—I think that our discrepancy here is not so much one of thoughts as of feelings. I *like* & greatly respect Moore; but that's all. He doesn't warm my heart (or very little), because what warms my heart most is human kindness, & Moore—*just like a child*—is not kind. He is kindly & he can be charming & nice to those he likes & he has great *depth*.—That's how it seems to me. If I'm wrong, I'm wrong.

He goes on to say in the same letter:

> My work is still going fairly well, though not as well as, say, 6

weeks ago. That's partly due to the fact that I've been a bit ill, &
also that a number of things are really worrying me.—Money is
not one of them. I am, of course, spending rather a lot, but I'll
have enough for another 2 years, I think. During that time, God
being willing, I'll get some work done; & that, after all, was why
I resigned my professorship. I mustn't worry about money *now*,
for if I did I couldn't work. (What will happen after that time I
don't yet know. Maybe I won't live that long anyway.)—One of
my present worries is the health of one of my sisters in Vienna.
She was operated on [for] cancer a short time ago & the operation, as far as it went, was successful, but she won't have *long* to
live. For that reason I *intend* to go to Vienna sometime next
spring; & that's got something to do with you, because if I go &
come back to England afterwards I intend to dictate the stuff
that I've been writing since last autumn, & *if* I do, I'll send you a
copy. May it act as manure on your field. [36]

He did actually bring me a copy of the writings last referred to
when he came to the States the following summer. This material is
incorporated in Part II of the *Investigations*.

In March 1949, Wittgenstein was still living in Ross's Hotel in
Dublin. My wife and I again urged him to visit us in America, to
which we received the following reply:

Thank you ever so much for the kind invitation. I got it almost a
week ago but I couldn't reply because my thoughts were in such
a turmoil; & even today I may not be able to produce anything
better than a jumble of incoherent sentences. First let me say a)
that I feel deeply grateful for your kindness & b) that I feel
strongly tempted to accept your invitation. But there are huge
difficulties.—My eldest sister is, to the best of my knowledge,
still alive & my two younger sisters *may* still want me to go to
Vienna before long. If this happened I'd probably go to Vienna
within the next 3 weeks & stay there for 3 or 4 weeks.—I went to
a travel agency to enquire about going to America & found out
that the journey there & back would cost me somewhere
between 80 & 120 pounds. Further I'm told that you alone will
have to pay for my upkeep in America, as I'm not allowed to take
with me more than £5. In fact I gather that you'd have to send
affidavits stating that you are able & willing to pay for all my
expences during my stay in the U.S.A. If these regulations did
not exist I could, theoretically, spend my own money in Amer-

ica, but in fact *I couldn't afford that*. I could afford the trip only by staying with you for *2 or 3 months* & sponging on you!—Now the prospect of staying with you for that length of time is very pleasant as far as I'm concerned, but there is the snag that I am an elderly man & aging pretty rapidly. I mean, physically, not, as far as I can see, mentally. . . . I imagine that you didn't quite realize all these snags when you invited me. Please take *everything* that I've said in this letter seriously & at it's face-value. [37]

I sent Wittgenstein the required affidavit and reassured him on the other points. In his next letter he announces that he has booked an ocean passage. He adds:

In this life one doesn't know what's going to happen; & so, supposing later on you were inclined, *for whatever reason*, to change your mind about the desirability of my visit, please *don't hesitate* to tell me so. . . . I haven't been doing any work at all for the last 2–3 weeks. My mind is tired & stale, partly, I think because I'm a bit exhausted, partly because lots of things worry me terribly just now. I think I could still discuss philosophy if I had someone here to discuss with, but alone I can't concentrate on it. [38]

In May he writes from Dublin:

I went to Vienna in the middle of April to see my eldest sister who is very ill. When I left 5 days ago she was still alive but there is no hope of her recovering. I arrived here last night. While I was in Vienna I was hardly able to write at all. I felt so rotten myself. I haven't done any work since the beginning of March & I haven't had the strength of even *trying* to do any. God knows how things will go on now. . . . I hope all of you are well, & I hope you won't find me a terribly disagreeable companion & bore when I come. [39]

In June, still at Dublin:

When I arrived here 3 weeks ago I went to see my doctor & he had my blood examined. They found that I had a severe anaemia of a rather unusual kind. It was suspected that I had a growth in my stomach but the x-ray definitely showed that there is no such thing inside me. I'm being given a lot of iron & liver extract & am getting better slowly. I think I shall certainly be able to sail with the Queen Mary on July 21st. There is, however, the question how far my anaemia will affect my ability to discuss. At present I am quite unable to do any philosophy & I don't think I'd be strong enough to have even a moderately decent discussion. In fact at present I'm *sure* I couldn't do it. But of course it's possible that by the end of July I may have recovered sufficiently for my brain to work again. . . . I *know* that you'd extend your hospitality to me even if I were *completely* dull & stupid, but *I* wouldn't want to be a mere dead weight in your house. I want to feel that I can at least give a *little* for so much kindness. [40]

When I suggested that he need not think of paying for his visit with philosophy he answered:

I never meant to *pay* for your kindness in discussions. Anyhow, the best I could give you would be lousy payment. All I meant was: I don't want to bore my kind hosts to *death*. However, let's not talk about it any more, especially as I've got good news: I've improved greatly during the last few days. So, obviously, the iron & the liver extract do work.

He went on to say that if I should not be able to meet him in New York he would 'jolly well' make the eight- or nine-hour train trip to Ithaca alone. 'Maybe, like in the films, I'll find a beautiful girl whom I meet on the boat & who will help me.' [41]

I went to New York to meet Wittgenstein at the ship. When I first saw him I was surprised at his apparent physical vigour. He was striding down the ramp with a pack on his back, a heavy suitcase in one hand, cane in the other. He was in very good spirits and not at all exhausted and he would not allow me to help him with his luggage. My chief recollection of the long train ride home is that we talked about music and that he whistled for me, with striking accuracy and expressiveness, some parts of Beethoven's 7th Symphony.

During the first month or six weeks that he lived with us his health was fairly good. He loved to go for walks in some nearby woods, with either my wife or myself. His stamina was surprising. On those walks he took a great interest in identifying the kinds of trees. One walk I remember particularly well. Wittgenstein wanted to determine the heights of the trees. Our procedure, invented by him, was that Wittgenstein would place himself at a sufficient distance from the tree to be measured, so that when he sighted along his arm and cane at the top of the tree, his arm was at an angle of roughly 45 degrees from the horizontal. I would pace off the distance from him to the foot of the tree, and a simple calculation gave us its approximate height. Wittgenstein directed this activity with real zest.

My wife once gave him some Swiss cheese and rye bread for lunch, which he greatly liked. Thereafter he would more or less insist on eating bread and cheese at all meals, largely ignoring the various dishes that my wife prepared. Wittgenstein declared that it did not much matter to him *what* he ate, so long as it was always the *same*. When a dish that looked especially appetizing was brought to the table, I sometimes exclaimed 'Hot Ziggety!'—a slang phrase that I learned as a boy in Kansas. Wittgenstein picked up this expression from me. It was inconceivably droll to hear him exclaim 'Hot Ziggety!' when my wife put the bread and cheese before him. During the first part of his visit Wittgenstein insisted on helping to wash the dishes after meals, and he was as before very fussy about the amount of soap and hot water that ought to be used and whether there was the right sort of dish mop. Once he rebuked me sternly for not rinsing properly. Before long, however, he left the dishes alone, and indeed his bodily strength so declined that he was not equal to that exertion.

One of Wittgenstein's favourite phrases was the exclamation, 'Leave the *bloody* thing *alone!*' He delivered this with a most emphatic intonation and mock solemnity of expression. It had roughly the signification that the thing in question was adequate and one should not try to improve it. He used it on a variety of occasions: one time meaning that the location of his bed was satisfactory and it should not be moved; another time, that the mending that my wife had done on a jacket of his was sufficient and that she should not try to make it better.

When the float in the toilet tank once failed to function, Wittgenstein took a lively interest in helping me to repair it. He had an obvious relish for a mechanical problem. When the repair was made, but I proposed adding one more adjustment, Wittgenstein stopped me with the words, 'Leave the *bloody* thing *alone!*' At Trinity College, Wittgenstein had taken me to look at one of the toilets in order to inspect its sturdy construction, and now he commented unfavourably on the construction of ours. He always had a keen appreciation of sound workmanship and a genuinely moral disapproval of the flimsy or the slipshod. He liked to think that there might be craftsmen who would insist on doing their jobs to *perfection*, and for no reason other than that that was the way it *ought* to be.

Soon after his arrival Wittgenstein proposed that he and I should read his book together. This we did for a few meetings, but again I found that activity too confining and not a satisfactory way of doing philosophy together; and I believe that Wittgenstein came to feel the same. He had numerous philosophical discussions that summer with various persons. With Oets Bouwsma and me he began to read Frege's paper 'Über Sinn und Bedeutung' (On sense and reference); and this led to two or three meetings in which Wittgenstein expounded his divergence from Frege. Then in one meeting we discussed free will and determinism. With Willis Doney and me he began to read the *Tractatus*, but this was not kept up. One anecdote should be recorded. I asked Wittgenstein whether, when he wrote the *Tractatus*, he had ever decided upon anything as an *example* of a 'simple object'. His reply was that at that time his thought had been that he was a *logician*; and that it was not his business, as a logician, to try to decide whether this thing or that was a simple thing or a complex thing, that being a purely *empirical* matter! It was clear that he regarded his former opinion as absurd.

With John Nelson, Doney, and myself, Wittgenstein met once to discuss a problem about memory. He met several times for discussions on various topics with some of my Cornell colleagues, among them Max Black and Stuart Brown, Bouwsma and myself also being present. In some of these meetings Wittgenstein showed the fire and vigour that was characteristic of him in Cambridge. Illness eventually stopped his attendance. At the beginning of the autumn term he met on two consecutive evenings with the Cornell graduate students of philosophy, once talking about verification, once about knowledge.

But the discussions that were of most value to me that summer were a series that took place between Wittgenstein and me, our topic being Moore's 'Proof of An External World' and also his 'Defence of Common Sense'. In particular, we talked about Moore's insistence that it is a correct use of language for him to say, when holding one of his hands before him, 'I *know* that this is a hand'; or to say, while pointing at a tree a few feet away, 'I *know* for *certain* that this is a *tree*!' In a published article I had maintained that this was a senseless use of 'know', and Moore had made a spirited reply to me in a letter. Wittgenstein and I discussed these matters in a number of conversations, he making many observations of the first importance about the concept of knowledge. The following is a brief account of them based on rough notes that I made:

There is a tendency to think of knowledge as a *mental state*. Now I am supposed to know my own mental states. If I say I have a certain mental state and do not have it, then I have told a lie. But I can say that I know so & so, and it can turn out that so & so is false; but it doesn't follow that I lied. Therefore, knowing is not a mental state.

Mental states, such as anxiety and pain, have degrees. *Certainty* also has degrees, e.g. 'How certain are you?' Since certainty has degrees we are helped to have the idea that knowledge is a mental state.

Moore would like to stare at a house that is only 20 feet away and say, with a peculiar intonation, 'I *know* that *there's* a *house!*' He does this because he wants to produce in himself the *feeling* of knowing. He wants to exhibit *knowing for certain* to himself. In this way he has the idea that he is replying to the sceptical philosopher who claims that everyday examples of knowing that there is a dog in the backyard, or that the neighbour's house is on fire, are not really or strictly *knowledge*, are not knowledge *in the highest degree*. It is as if someone had said 'You don't really feel pain when you are pinched' and Moore then pinched himself in order to feel the pain, and thus prove to himself that the other is wrong. Moore treats the sentence 'I know so & so' like the sentence 'I have a pain.' The criterion that he knows that so & so will be that he *says* that he does.

Physical-object statements, like 'That's a tree', sometimes play a role similar to that of mathematical propositions, in the respect that experience could not refute them. If I walked over to that tree and could touch nothing I might lose confidence in everything my senses told me, just as I might lose confidence in all calculations if some simple addition kept coming out differently. Moore said 'I *know* that there's a tree', partly because of the feeling that if it turned out *not* to be a tree, he would have to 'give up'.

I might refuse to regard anything as *evidence* that there isn't a tree. If I were to walk over to it and to feel nothing at all, I might say that I was *then* deluded, not that I was previously mistaken in thinking it a tree. If I say that I would not *call* anything 'evidence' against that's being a tree, then I am not making a psychological prediction—but a *logical* statement.

In the ordinary use of 'know' it is always sensible to speak of 'making sure'. Now Moore says, e.g. 'I know that this is a shoe' in circumstances where it doesn't have any sense to 'make sure'. And this may actually be a reason for his insistence on saying 'I know' in this case. He may be wishing to say that there can't be any such thing as a further 'making sure' that this is a shoe; and that if there could be a further 'making sure' what better would it give me than what I now have. We have to come to a stop! If there is a making sure *here*, then there is no making sure at all! Moore's statement 'I *know* that this is a shoe' may amount to saying: 'There isn't any *making sure* that this is a shoe; and no matter what might happen I shouldn't call it evidence against this being a shoe.'

Instead of saying that Moore's statement 'I know that this is a tree' is a misuse of language, it is better to say that it has no clear meaning, and that Moore himself doesn't know how he is using it. We can *suspect* that he is using it to make some philosophical point, e.g. that some physical-object statements function like mathematical statements; or the point that it is a misusage of language to say 'Perhaps it is not a tree.' But Moore himself isn't clear what he means by it. It isn't even clear to him that he is not giving it an ordinary usage. He is confused by the difference between using it in some ordinary sense and using it to make a philosophical point.

At this stage of our discussion Wittgenstein came to the conclusion that, contrary to what he had previously said, it is *false* that 'In the ordinary use of "know" it is always sensible to speak of "making sure" ':

There is an ordinary use of 'I know' when there isn't any *making sure*. E.g. a sighted person could say it to a blind man who asks 'Are you sure that it's a tree?' And also when we have *completed* an investigation we can say, 'I know now that it's a tree.' Another example: if you and I were coming through woods towards a house and I broke out into the clearing and there was the house right before me, I might exclaim 'There's the house.' You, back in the bushes, might ask doubtfully 'Are you sure?', and I should reply 'I *know* it.' Here the use of 'I know it' would be natural, and yet it would also be a case of certainty 'in the highest degree', a case in which I should be willing to count nothing as evidence that there isn't a house there.

Moore might have given such examples, examples of a use of 'I know' in which that expression really functions 'im sprachlichen Verkehr' i.e. in the actual traffic of language, in 'the stream of life'. But he doesn't give such examples: he prefers to gaze at a tree and say 'I *know* there's a tree there.' And this is because he wants to give himself the *experience* of knowing.

We might say 'A human being knows that he has two hands' and mean by this, that he doesn't have to count them or make sure that there are still two—whereas some other creatures might have hands that occasionally disappeared.

'The earth has existed for one million years' has sense; 'The earth has existed for five minutes' is nonsense. What if someone argued that the latter has sense because it is *implied* by the former?

Are not some of Moore's 'truisms' more absurd than others? It isn't difficult to think of usages for 'I know that this is a hand'; it is more difficult for 'I know that the earth has existed for many years'; it is still more difficult for 'I know that I am a human being.' To understand a sentence is to be prepared for one of its uses. If we can't think of any use for it at all, then we don't understand it at all.

Experiential propositions do not all have the same logical status. With regard to some, of which we say that we *know* them to be true, we can imagine circumstances on the basis of which we should say that the statement had turned out to be false. But with others there are no circumstances in which we should say 'it turned out to be false.' This is a logical remark and has nothing to do with what I shall say ten minutes from now.

Moore's propositions—'I know that I am a human being', 'I know that the earth has existed for many years', etc.—have this characteristic, that it is impossible to think of circumstances in which we should allow that we have evidence against them. But when the sceptical philosophers say 'You don't know' and Moore replies 'I do know', his reply is quite useless, unless it is to assure them that he, Moore, doesn't feel any doubt whatever. But that is not what is at issue.

These philosophers want to make a *logical* point. They want to say we don't know something to be true if future experience can disprove it. There are kinds of statements that future experience cannot refute, e.g. sense-datum statements, and mathematical or logical statements. To use 'I know' with sense-datum statements is silly. It adds nothing. In mathematics it isn't silly. And there is a close resemblance between some experiential statements and mathematical ones—namely, future experience won't provide reasons for rejecting them.

The sceptical philosophers want to say that with experiential statements, 'I know it' is the same as 'I believe it and it is true.' They think that degree of *certainty* is degree of *conviction*. They interpret Moore's 'I know it with absolute certainty' as an expression of extreme conviction. What is needed is to show them that the highest degree of certainty is nothing psychological but something logical: that there is a point at which there is neither any 'making more certain' nor any 'turning out to be false'. Some experimental statements have this property. Some others are related in various ways to those that have this property. Thus we can give a logical justification of the use of 'I know' with experiential statements.

In teaching words to a child one does not say either 'I *believe* that that is red' or 'I *know* that that is red,' but simply 'That is red.' If one's teaching was always expressed with *doubt*, it is difficult to say whether the child would learn anything. He certainly would not learn to express himself *with reservations.* Unless words like 'red' and 'chair' are learned there isn't any language.

Proofs in mathematics involve the writing of equations on paper and seeing that one expression is contained in another. But if it is always to be doubted what expressions appear on a paper, then there can't be any proofs or any mathematics.

It could happen sometimes that my senses deceived me, but not all the time. Hallucinations must be the exception. A physical-object judgement turning out to be false must be the exception.

Moore's attempt to find a difference in his experience between 'knowing' and 'being certain' is like this: that I should say that I see something different when I see Wittgenstein in a mirror from what I see when I see *myself* in a mirror.

Certain propositions belong to my 'frame of reference'. If I had to give *them* up, I shouldn't be able to judge *anything*. Take the example of the earth's having existed for many years before I was born. What evidence against it could there be? A document?

Doubt, belief, certainty—like feelings, emotions, pain, etc.— have characteristic facial expressions. Knowledge does *not* have a characteristic facial expression. There is a *tone* of doubt, and a tone of conviction, but no tone of knowledge.[6]

The foregoing notes are not intended to be verbatim, although some phrases and sentences actually are verbatim. The notes were written up a day or two after each talk. They are a condensed summary of what I took away from a number of discussions, occurring over a period of several weeks. A few of the thoughts may have been my own, but certainly most were not. I believe that these notes give a reasonably accurate report of part, although certainly not all, that Wittgenstein said. Nonetheless I wish to issue an emphatic warning that they do not pretend to give an authentic version of his thoughts. One remark of his struck me then, as it does now, as being especially noteworthy and as summing up a good deal of his philosophy. It is 'Ein Ausdruck hat nur im Strome des Lebens Bedeutung' (An expression has meaning only in the stream of life). Wittgenstein believed that this aphorism was written down in one of his manuscripts; and perhaps it is, but not in any that I have seen.[7]

On one of our walks Wittgenstein said that if he had the money he thought he would have his book (Part I of the *Investigations*) mimeographed and distributed among his friends. He said that it was not in a completely finished state, but that he did not think that he could give the final polish to it in his lifetime. This plan would have the merit that he could put in parentheses after a remark, expressions of dissatisfaction, like 'This is not quite right' or 'This is fishy.' He would like to put his book into the hands of his friends, but to take it to a publisher right then was out of the question. He asked me what I thought of this idea of mimeographing it. I replied that I did not like it at all. Wittgenstein was angered by my remark. He suggested that, like other students of his, I was reluctant to see his work made public because people would then know where my own philosophical ideas came from. What I had felt was not what he supposed, but rather that it was not fitting

---

[6] See Additional Note 2 on p. 83.
[7] See Additional Note 3 on p. 84.

that a book of that importance should be distributed in mimeo-graph: instead it should be bound in 'leather and gold'.

More than once, Wittgenstein said to me that it was a problem for him as to what to do with the remainder of his life. 'When a person has only one thing in the world—namely, a certain talent—what is he to do when he begins to lose that talent?' he asked. Wittgenstein spoke so earnestly and sombrely that I, knowing that three of his brothers had committed suicide, feared that he might attempt the same.

The weather was unusually hot that summer and Wittgenstein's room on the second floor was often very uncomfortable. He once pointed out to me that the wire mesh of the window screens restricted to some extent the movement of air through his win-dows, and wondered why they could not be removed. I replied that if this were done great numbers of insects would enter and prove even more disagreeable than the heat. Wittgenstein doubted that this was so. He remarked that in England and on the Continent windows were commonly left unscreened. I answered that there were more insects in America. Wittgenstein didn't believe this, and when he went out for a walk later that day he made a point of looking at a number of houses in order to see whether their win-dows were screened. He found that all of them were but, oddly enough, instead of inferring that there must be a good reason for it, he concluded with some irritation that Americans were the vic-tims of widespread and unthinking prejudice as to the necessity of window screens!

Wittgenstein became extremely ill during the latter part of his stay with us. He had a painful bursitis in both shoulders, was unable to sleep, and was extremely weak. His doctor arranged for him to spend two days in the hospital to obtain a complete physical examination. On the day before he went to the hospital he was not only ill, but also frightened. He had told me previously that his father died of cancer and, in addition, his favourite sister was gradually dying of the same disease, despite several operations. Wittgenstein's fear was not that he would be found to have cancer (he was quite prepared for that) but that he might be kept at the hospital for surgery. His fear of surgery came near to panic. It was not the operation itself he dreaded, but to become a useless and bed-ridden invalid whose death had only been deferred for a little. He was also very afraid that the doctors might prevent him from making the return passage to England in October, which was already booked. 'I don't want to die in America. I am a European—I want to die in Europe,' he murmured to me in a frenzy. And he exclaimed: 'What a fool I was to come.'

He returned from the hospital in quite a cheerful frame of mind. The examination had not found anything seriously wrong with him (although later that autumn he was discovered to have cancer); and there was no longer any threat of his being detained in the hospital or of his departure for England being postponed. I did not see how he could make the trip since he was so extremely weak: but in the two weeks before he sailed he recovered strength in a surprising way.

Wittgenstein returned to England in October. Early in December I received the following letter from Cambridge:

> The doctors have now made their diagnosis. I have cancer of the prostate. But this sounds, in a way, much worse than it is, for there is a drug (actually some hormones) which can, as I'm told, alleviate the symptoms of the disease so that I *can* live on for years. The doctor even tells me that I may be able to work again, but I can't imagine that. I was in no way shocked when I heard I had cancer, but I *was* when I heard that one could do something about it, because I had *no* wish to live on. But I couldn't have my wish. I am treated with great kindness by everyone & I have an immensely kind doctor who isn't a fool either. [44]

A few days later he asked me to 'not *under any circumstances* let *any* one know about the nature of my illness who doesn't already know about it. . . . This is of the greatest importance for me as I plan to go to Vienna for Christmas & *not* to let my family know about the real disease.' [45]

Wittgenstein went to Vienna in December, and remained until the end of March. A letter in January says that he is very well and not at all depressed. He remarks how extremely lucky he was that his illness was not correctly diagnosed in America. He adds:

> My brain works very sluggishly these days but I can't say I mind. I'm reading various odds & ends, e.g. Goethe's Theory of colour which, with all its absurdities, has very interesting points, & stimulates me to think. . . . I'm not writing at all because my thoughts never sufficiently crystallize. Not that it matters. [47]

In April 1950 he was back in England. He had received an invitation to give the John Locke lectures in Oxford, for which he would receive two hundred pounds. But there would be an audience of 200 and the lectures would have to be quite formal and there could be no discussion. He declined this invitation and the reason he gave to me was, 'I don't think I can give formal lectures to a large audience that would be any good.' That spring I succeeded in interesting a director of the Rockefeller Foundation, Chadbourne Gilpatrick, in the possibility of awarding Wittgenstein a research grant. I informed Wittgenstein of this and, after thanking me for undertaking it, he replied:

The thought of being able to live where I like, of not having to be a burden or a nuisance to others, of doing philosophy when my nature inclines me to do it is, of course, pleasant for me, as it would be for anyone else who wants to do philosophy. But I could not accept money from the Rockefeller Foundation unless the directors knew the complete truth about me. The truth is this. a) I have not been able to do any sustained good work since the beginning of March 1949. b) Even before that date I could not work *well* for more than 6 or 7 months a year. c) As I'm getting older my thoughts become markedly less forceful & crystallize more rarely & I get tired very much more easily. d) My health is in a somewhat labile state owing to a constant slight anaemia which inclines me to catch infections. This further diminishes the chance of my doing really good work. e) Though it's impossible for me to make any definite predictions, it seems to me likely that my mind will never again work as vigorously as it did, say, 14 months ago. f) I cannot promise to publish anything during my lifetime.

I believe that as long as I live & as often as the state of my mind permits it I will think about philosophical problems & try to write about them. I also believe that much of what I wrote in the past 15 or 20 years may be of interest to people when it's published. But it is, nevertheless, perfectly possible that *all* that I'm *going* to produce will be flat, uninspired & uninteresting. There are many examples of people who did excellent work when they were young, & *very* dull work indeed when they got old.

I think this is all I can say about it. I believe you should show this letter to the director you approached about me. It is obviously impossible to accept a grant under false pretences, & you *may* unintentionally have presented my case in too rosy a light. [50]

During part of 1950, Wittgenstein lived in Oxford in Miss Anscombe's home. In July he wrote: 'I have hardly any philosophical
discussions. I could see students if I wanted, but I don't want to.
I've got all sorts of unclear thoughts in my old head which perhaps
will remain there forever in this unsatisfactory state.' Oets
Bouwsma and his family spent that year in Oxford. Wittgenstein
used to visit them and loved eating Mrs. Bouwsma's home-made
apple-sauce. In a letter to me he remarked of his inability to do philosophical work, 'I am just good enough to eat apple-sauce with a
philosopher.'

In the autumn of 1950, Wittgenstein went to Norway for five
weeks with a companion who fell ill twice with bronchitis during
that period:

> So there was no end of trouble . . . I had intended to do some
> work but I didn't do any. I may possibly go back to Norway
> before long & try to work. It's the only place I know where I can
> have real quiet. Of course it's possible that I'm no longer able to
> do any decent research, but it's certainly worth while finding out
> if I am or not. [52]

Wittgenstein later wrote that he had arranged to spend the winter on the farm of a friend in Norway and had booked a passage for
December 30th but had to cancel the trip because of illness. In
January of 1951 he writes that Gilpatrick of the Rockefeller Foundation has been to visit him.

> I told him what I wrote to you some months ago, i.e., that in my
> present state of health & intellectual dullness I couldn't accept a
> grant; but I said that if, against all probability & hope, I should
> one day find that I could again do worthwhile work in philo-
> sophy, I'd write to him. And so we parted on friendly terms.

He goes on to say that Oxford 'is a philosophical desert'. (It was
reported to me that Wittgenstein had also referred to the philosophical circles of Oxford as 'the influenza area', a remark that gave
offence to some Oxford dons.) He adds: 'My mind's completely
dead. This isn't a complaint, for I don't really suffer from it. I know
that life must have an end once & that mental life can cease before
the rest does.' [54]

Soon after this he went to Cambridge to stay in the home of his
physician, Dr. Bevan. (When Wittgenstein first learned from Dr.

Bevan that he had cancer, he expressed an extreme aversion and even fear of spending his last days in a hospital. Dr. Bevan then told him that he could come to his house to die. Wittgenstein was deeply grateful for this remarkable offer.) He had previously been very ill in Oxford, but was now better, although still not well. 'I can't even *think* of work at present, & it doesn't matter, if only I don't live too long! I'm not depressed though.' [55] He remained at Dr. Bevan's until his death. In March he writes that he is feeling much better and suffering hardly any pain. 'I am of course very weak & there seems no doubt that this isn't going to change for the better as time goes on. I hardly think that I'll be on this earth when you come to Cambridge in Autumn '52. Still, one doesn't know. I am not depressed in the least, by the way.' Two months previously he had sent me the biography of Rommel by Brigadier Young. In this same letter he remarks 'I'm very glad you like the Rommel book. I looked at it quite recently again & was impressed again by the thoroughly *decent* way in which it's written. Such books are few & far between.'[56]

The last letter that I received from Wittgenstein was written 13 days before his death. He says:

> An extraordinary thing happened to me. About a month ago I suddenly found myself in the right frame of mind for doing philosophy. I had been *absolutely* certain that I'd never again be able to do it. It's the first time after more than 2 years that the curtain in my brain has gone up.—Of course, so far I've only worked for about 5 weeks & it may be all over by tomorrow; but it bucks me up a lot now.

He also says that 'apart from a certain weakness which has constant ups & downs I'm feeling *very* well these days'. [57]

When Wittgenstein came to live with the Bevans, Mrs. Bevan was at first frightened of him, but soon became devoted. They took many walks together. As she told me, his influence over her came to be great, even in little things. For example, she had bought a new coat to wear to a party, and before leaving the house, went to show it to Wittgenstein. He scrutinized it carefully, said 'Wait!' in a peremptory tone, took a pair of scissors and, without asking permission, cut several large buttons off the front. And she liked the coat better that way!

Wittgenstein was feeling extremely well and working furiously.

At the time when 'the curtain went up' he said to Mrs. Bevan: 'I am going to work now as I have never worked before!'

On Friday, April 27th, he took a walk in the afternoon. That night he fell violently ill. He remained conscious and when informed by the doctor that he could live only a few days, he exclaimed 'Good!' Before losing consciousness he said to Mrs. Bevan (who was with him throughout the night) 'Tell them I've had a wonderful life!' By 'them' he undoubtedly meant his close friends. When I think of his profound pessimism, the intensity of his mental and moral suffering, the relentless way in which he drove his intellect, his need for love together with the harshness that repelled love, I am inclined to believe that his life was fiercely unhappy. Yet at the end he himself exclaimed that it had been 'wonderful'! To me this seems a mysterious and strangely moving utterance.[8]

[8] See Additional Note 4 on p. 84.

ADDITIONAL NOTES (1983)

1 (p. 60). I think that the question of whether Wittgenstein was 'a religious person' is even more difficult than I realized at the time I wrote the *Memoir*. At that time I had no knowledge of the vast number of remarks that he had written in his notebooks on many subjects, remarks that do not belong to his strictly philosophical writings. These remarks were collected by Georg Henrik von Wright. A small selection of them was first published under the title *Vermischte Bemerkungen* (Miscellaneous Remarks), edited by G. H. von Wright in collaboration with Heikki Nyman (Suhrkamp Verlag, Frankfurt am Main, 1977). An amended second edition was published with an English translation by Peter Winch, under the title *Culture and Value* (Blackwell, Oxford, 1980).

Many of the remarks are *about* religion: but some of them can be regarded as *religious thoughts*. For example, in 1937 Wittgenstein wrote:

> Christianity is not a doctrine, not, I mean, a theory about what has happened and will happen to the human soul, but a description of something that actually takes place in human life. For 'consciousness of sin' is a real event, and so are despair and salvation through faith. Those who speak of such things (Bunyan, for instance) are simply describing what has happened to them, whatever anyone may want to say about it. (*Culture and Value*, p. 28)

In 1944 he wrote:

> The Christian religion is only for one who needs infinite help, that is, only for one who feels infinite anguish. The whole earth can suffer no greater torment than a *single* soul. The Christian faith—as I see it—is one's refuge in this *ultimate* torment. Anyone to whom it is given in this anguish to open his heart, instead of contracting it, accepts the means of salvation in his heart. (ibid., p. 46)

In 1946:

> I believe that one of the things Christianity says is that sound doctrines are all useless. That you have to change your *life*. (Or the *direction* of your life.) It says that all wisdom is cold; and that you can no more use it for setting your life to rights than you can forge *cold* iron. A correct doctrine need not *take hold* of you; you can follow it as you would a doctor's prescription.—But here you need something to grasp you and turn you around.—I.e. this is how I understand it.) Once you have been turned around, you must *stay* turned round. Wisdom is without passion. Faith, by contrast, is what Kierkegaard calls a *passion*. (ibid., p. 53)

Another important source of information about Wittgenstein's religious thoughts and feelings is M. O'C. Drury's account of his conversations with Wittgenstein. (In *Recollections of Wittgenstein*, edited by Rush Rhees, Oxford University Press, 1984.) On one occasion Wittgenstein told Drury that he had received a letter from an old friend in Austria, who was a priest. Wittgenstein remarked:

> In it he says he hopes my work will go well, if it should be God's will. Now that is all I want: if it should be God's will. Bach wrote on the title page of his *Orgelbuchlein*, 'To the glory of the most high God, and that my neighbour may be benefited thereby.' That is what I would have liked to say about my work. (op. cit., p. 168)

When talking to Drury about his philosophical writings, Wittgenstein said: 'I am not a religious man but I cannot help seeing every problem from a religious point of view.' Drury observes (rightly, I think) that such a remark raises the question 'as to whether there are not dimensions in Wittgenstein's thought that are still largely being ignored?' (ibid., p. 79).

I have quoted here a few samples of Wittgenstein's many written thoughts and recorded remarks that bear a religious stamp. If to be 'a religious person' means to lead 'a religious life', then I think he was not a religious person. Yet he reflected often and deeply on what it would mean to live such a life. He was dismayed by his own character, perceiving himself as vain, cowardly, false. Sometimes he suffered the anguish that has pushed others into a religious life. Probably he had no real hope that his life would take a new direction, that he would be 'turned around'. Probably he felt that he *could* not, or *would* not, 'open his heart'. At times he felt a dread of the Last Judgment—as when he wrote to me, 'May I prove not too much of a skunk when I shall be tried.' [3]

Thus, if it is right to say that Wittgenstein was not a religious person, there must be weighed against this the fact that his reflections about himself and mankind, and even about the aims of his intensive philosophical work, were penetrated by thoughts and feelings of a religious character.

2 (p. 75). It was not until after the publication of the *Memoir* in 1958 that I learned that Wittgenstein wrote extensively on the topics of these discussions that he and I had in Ithaca in the Summer of 1949. Some of this writing was on loose sheets, undated; the remainder in small notebooks, containing dates. Apparently all of this material was written in the last year and a half of Wittgenstein's life. He had no opportunity to revise or polish it. The last entry was two days before his death on April 29, 1951.

This work was published in 1969 under the title *On Certainty* (*Über Gewissheit*). It was edited by G. E. M. Anscombe and G. H. von Wright, with English translation by Denis Paul and G. E. M. Anscombe (Blackwell, Oxford, 1969).

On Certainty is a brilliant illustration of the novelty of Wittgenstein's thinking. The concepts of *certainty* and *knowledge* have received a vast amount of study in the history of philosophy. Wittgenstein presents an entirely fresh way of viewing these concepts.

There are striking similarities between *On Certainty* and the ideas that Wittgenstein first began to formulate in our conversations in Ithaca: but Wittgenstein's written remarks advance these topics into areas of thought that were not touched upon in those conversations.

3 (p. 75). In one of Wittgenstein's manuscripts written in the spring of 1949 there occurs the sentence 'Nur im Fluss des Lebens haben die Worte ihre Bedeutung' (Words have their meaning only in the flow of life). This sentence is on p. 118 of a volume of Wittgenstein's writings entitled *Last Writings on the Philosophy of Psychology*, edited by G. H. von Wright and Heikki Nyman and translated by C. F. Luckhardt and M. A. E. Aue (Blackwell, Oxford, 1982).

4 (p. 81). I have had second thoughts about my remark that Wittgenstein's life was 'fiercely unhappy'. For one thing, he gained many friends: people who not only admired him but loved him. And he was their true friend, always concerned for their health and well-being. These friendships were surely a source of richness in his life.

For another thing, he was engaged in prolonged and intensive intellectual work. The notebooks, manuscripts, and typescripts produced between 1929 and 1951 come to a total of roughly thirty thousand pages. Throughout this vast material are innumerable thoughts of great power and beauty. His writing is everywhere stamped with originality—with striking turns of thought and dazzling similes. Typically he was dissatisfied with what he wrote. Nevertheless, he was continually arriving at fresh insights, seeing connections between one region of thought and another, spotting false analogies, trying out new ways of tackling the problems that have kept philosophy in turmoil for many centuries. I find it impossible to believe that this activity of creation and discovery gave him no delight, even though he always felt that it came short of what was needed. In a letter to me in 1943 he said that philosophical work is 'the only work that's given me real satisfaction. No other work really bucks me up.' [7] In a manuscript of 1931 he wrote: 'Die Freude an meinem Gedanken ist die Freude an meinem eigenen seltsamen Leben.' (The joy of my thoughts is the joy of my own strange life.) So, though there was plenty of pain there was also joy—and much that was 'wonderful'.

WITTGENSTEIN'S
LETTERS

TO NORMAN MALCOLM

NOTE

I received fifty-seven letters from Wittgenstein over a period of eleven years (1940–51). The letters are given in full except for the omission of a few names (indicated by long dashes) to avoid possible offence or embarrassment. Three of the letters were addressed to my wife; four of them to us jointly. I have numbered the letters in chronological order and in some cases added comments as endnotes.

From 1936 to 1938 I was at Harvard University as a postgraduate student of philosophy. I received permission from the Faculty of Philosophy to spend the following year at Cambridge University in order to study with Professor G. E. Moore. I arrived there in the autumn of 1938 and Moore agreed to supervise the doctoral dissertation that I was to present to Harvard. I had been an admirer of Moore's philosophical writings, especially the essays in his *Philosophical Studies*, ever since Oets Bouwsma introduced me to them when I was a student of his at the University of Nebraska. About Wittgenstein I knew nothing. At Harvard he was regarded as a mysterious figure who was supposed to be the guiding spirit of the Vienna Circle and also a dangerously nihilistic influence in philosophy. It was known that he was the author of the *Tractatus Logico-Philosophicus*: but I don't believe that this work was studied at Harvard at that time. Something of the Harvard attitude towards Wittgenstein is conveyed by the following anecdote: Before departing for England I went to say goodbye to Henry Sheffer, the logician. He said to me, in a mocking tone, that when I met Wittgenstein, I should make a low bow and exclaim, 'There is but one Tautology and Wittgenstein is its Prophet!'

My first observation of Wittgenstein is recorded in my Memoir (p. 23). I attended his lectures and discussions throughout the academic year 1939, and we became friends. In February 1940 I returned to the USA whereupon our correspondence began.

I Trinity College
Cambridge
26.3.40

Dear Malcolm,

Your letter & the magazines[1] arrived here simultaneously a day or two ago. I found them here today on returning from a week end excursion to Hastings. Thanks awfully! I'm sure they're grand. My critical eye can see that without having read them, because my critical eye is an X-ray eye & can penetrate from 2 to 4000 pages. That's in fact how I got all my learning. Now please take it easy! One magazine a month is *ample*. If you send me more I won't have time to do any philosophy. Also please don't waste your money on mags for me, & see that *you* get enough to eat! I'm glad to say Smythies has got unconditional exemption.[2] I shall give him your regards when I see him tomorrow & as I know that he'll send you his I give them to you right now. My lectures have gone moderately well this term & I hope they won't be too awful next term. I'm feeling a bit run down just now. I'm extremely glad that you've found kind people to stay with.[3] I wish you lots of good & decent thoughts.

Yours affectionately
Ludwig Wittgenstein

[1] Wittgenstein was fond of short detective stories, especially those published in a detective story magazine by the American firm Street & Smith.

[2] The Second World War had begun in 1939. Yorick Smythies, a student and close friend of Wittgenstein, and also a friend of mine, was exempted from military service as a conscientious objector.

[3] When I returned to Harvard in the spring of 1940 I had no money and no job. Professor and Mrs. C. I. Lewis generously invited me to live with them for a few months while I was completing my doctoral dissertation.

2 Trinity College
Cambridge
29.5.40

My dear Malcolm,

Thanks for the magazines. They're grand but, of course, not *as* grand as 'Detective Story' mags. I wonder why you tried to be original instead of sticking to the good, old, tried out stuff.[1]—My lectures didn't go *too* bad this term, & last week I had an 'at-home' &

I'm intending to have at-homes regularly now because I have an idea it might steady people a bit if they go on with *some sort of* decent thinking *in spite* of the unrest they feel. Of course if people should cease to come that'll be just that. Smythies is still in Cambridge, &, for my *own* sake, I'm glad he is. Moore[2] isn't looking too well these days. I saw him this morning & he was as nice as ever.

Good luck!!

Affectionately

Ludwig Wittgenstein

[1] Apparently I had sent a different brand of detective 'mags'.
[2] Professor G. E. Moore.

3

Trinity College

Cambridge

22.6.40.

My dear Malcolm,

Thanks for your letter dated May 31st & for the 1½d. They'll come in very handy. Congratulations to your Ph.D.![1] And now: may you make good use of it! By that I mean: may you not cheat either yourself or your students. Because, unless I'm very much mistaken, *that's* what will be expected from you. And it will be *very* difficult not to do it, & perhaps impossible; & in this case: may you have the strength *to quit*.

This ends today's sermon.—I've had a good deal of worry lately as Skinner,[2] about a month ago, fell ill with something called 'glandular fever' of which he's only now recovering slowly.—I saw Moore the other day & his health is all right & he is in quite good spirits.—I have found it almost impossible to work for many weeks, & I have therefore arranged with Lewy[3] that I'll give him every day an hour or two of talk on the foundations of math's & similar subject. It doesn't do him any harm & it helps me & seems to be the only way just now to get my brain moving a little. It's a shame—but there it is.—Smythies has gone down & I don't know exactly where he is but I hope to hear from him soon.

May I not prove too much of a skunk when I shall be tried.[4]

I wish you good (not necessarily clever) thoughts, & decency that won't come out in the wash.

Affectionately

Ludwig Wittgenstein

If Skinner knew that I was writing to you I know he'ld like me to send you his best wishes, so here they are: ....

[1] I had informed Wittgenstein that I received this degree from Harvard in June 1940.

[2] Francis Skinner had been a student of mathematics at Cambridge. He attended Wittgenstein's lectures for several years. When I met Skinner in 1939 he had given up a career in mathematics (perhaps due to Wittgenstein's influence) and was working, I believe, for the Cambridge Instrument Company. Probably he was Wittgenstein's closest friend. They went on long walks on weekends and sometimes spent holidays together, one in Norway, another in Ireland. Skinner's sudden death from illness in 1941 was a great blow for Wittgenstein.

[3] Casimir Lewy, a research student of philosophy at Cambridge and a friend of mine. Later he was Lecturer in Philosophy at Cambridge and a Fellow of Trinity College.

[4] This remark does not refer to any previous or subsequent context of the Letters, nor to any secular trial or examination. I believe it meant: 'when I shall be tried at the Last Judgment'.

4

Trinity College
Cambridge
3.10.40.

Dear Malcolm:

Thanks for your letter, dated Sept. 9th. I was glad to hear from you. It'll be fine to get detective mags from you. There is a terrible scarcity of them now. My mind feels all underfed.—As a matter of fact I've been feeling pretty rotten most of this summer. Partly because of bad health, partly because my brain was no d . . . good at all & I couldn't work. I'm feeling a bit better now. That's to say, my health is *entirely* all right & my mind seems a little more active. But God knows how long that'll last. I wish you good luck; in particular with your work at the university.[1] The temptation for you to cheat yourself will be OVERWHELMING (though I don't mean more for you than for anyone else in your position.). *Only by a miracle* will you be able to do decent work in teaching philosophy. Please remember these words, even if you forget everything I've ever said to you; &, if you can help it, don't think that I'm a crank because nobody else will say this to you.—I haven't heard from Smythies for about 4 months. I don't know why he doesn't write nor where he is, or anything. I see very few people these days. Skinner is almost the only person I see regularly. He has to work long hours but he's in good health. I don't see Wisdom[2] at all. I've heard from a friend of mine in Montreal about Mrs. Wisdom.[3] I think she's all right.—Good luck!

Affectionately
Ludwig Wittgenstein

1 I was an Instructor of Philosophy at Princeton University.
2 John Wisdom was Lecturer in Philosophy at Cambridge and a Fellow of Trinity College. Later he was Professor of Philosophy at Cambridge. I went to his lectures in 1938–9, and had many discussions with him, and we became friends.
3 Mrs. John Wisdom, whom I knew, and about whom I had inquired.

5   Trinity College
                                             Cambridge
                                             5.7.41.

Dear Malcolm,

I got your letter dated May 17th yesterday. It's always good to hear from you! I am sorry—*honestly*—that you find you won't be able to teach at Princeton after next year.[1] You know what my opinion of teaching philosophy is & I haven't changed it; but I like you to quit for the *right* reasons, not for the wrong ones ('right' & 'wrong' as *I* can see it.). I know you'll make a good soldier;[2] still, I hope you won't have to be one. I wish you could live quiet, in a sense, & be in a position to be kind & *understanding* to all sorts of human beings who *need* it! Because we all need this sort of thing very badly. The mags arrived a few weeks ago & I immediately thanked you for them. They were *really* grand!—Skinner sends his regards & Smythies will, when he hears from me. I wish I could dine with you before long! Lots of good wishes!

                                   Affectionately
                                   Ludwig Wittgenstein

1 I had been reappointed at Princeton for the academic year 1941–2, but had been informed that this would terminate my appointment.
2 In the Summer of 1941 I had written to Wittgenstein that I would not be reappointed at Princeton for 1942–3, but had added that it didn't matter since the US would soon be in the war and I would probably enlist in the US Army.

6   Nuffield House
                                             Guy's Hospital[1]
                                             London S.E.1.
                                             24.11.42

Dear Malcolm,

I was *glad* to get your letter, dated Oct. 30. I enclose a foul copy of a very wonderful German novel.[2] I couldn't get a decent copy—at least I had no time to look for a better one. German books, as you can imagine, are very difficult to get these days. You may find it rather difficult to read, &, of course, you mayn't like it; but I hope you will. It's a sort of a Christmas present & I hope you won't mind it being so dirty. The advantage of this is that you can read it down in the engine-room[3] without making it *more* dirty. If you find you like it I'll try to get you the book of which this is only one story. There are five of them called: 'Zuricher Novellen', because they're all in some way connected with Zurich: Keller was a Swiss, & one of the greatest German *prose* writers.—As I told you in my last letter I haven't heard from Smythies for ages & have an idea that he has stopped being interested in me. But perhaps it isn't so.—Wisdom is still in Cambridge. I never see him.—Let me hear from you again. Bless you!!

Affectionately
Ludwig Wittgenstein

[1] I believe it was late in 1941, or in 1942, that Wittgenstein stopped lecturing in Cambridge and became a dispensary porter in Guy's Hospital, London. M. O'C. Drury records that one of Wittgenstein's duties was to prepare Lassar's ointment for the dermatological department, and that the sister on the ward declared that no one before had produced Lassar's ointment of such high quality! (Drury's memoirs of Wittgenstein are contained in the book *Recollections of Wittgenstein*, edited by Rush Rhees (Oxford University Press, Oxford, 1984)).

[2] Wittgenstein sent me Gottfried Keller's *Hadlaub*, the first of the Zuricher Novellen.

[3] In the spring of 1942 I enlisted in the US Navy. At the time of this letter I was serving on a patrol vessel in the Caribbean, but not 'down in the engine-room'.

---

7   Clinical Research Lab.
                                          Royal Victoria Infirmary[1]
                                          Newcastle on Tyne
                                          11.9.43.

Dear Malcolm,

I haven't written to you for a long time & haven't heard from you for ages.

19.9.43. These line I wrote a week ago & then was interrupted. The next day your letter arrived. I was *very* glad to hear from you. It would be ever so good to see you again.[2] I too regret that for external & internal reasons I can't do philosophy, for that's the only work that's given me real satisfaction. No other work really bucks me up. I'm extremely busy now & my mind is kept occupied the whole time but at the end of the day I just feel tired & sad.—Well, *perhaps* better times will come again.—I haven't heard from Smythies for *many* months. I know he is in Oxford but he doesn't write to me.—Lewy is still at Cambridge, which, I'm sure, is very

bad for him & not good for anyone else. Rhees[3] is still lecturing at
Swansea & as good as ever. I very rarely come to Cambridge now,
about once every three months. I've given up my rooms in College.
I'm supposed, of course, to come back there as a professor after the
war, but I must say I can't quite imagine how I'll be able to do it. I
wonder if I'll ever be able to teach philosophy again regularly. I
rather think I shan't be able.

I hope you'll see Moore[4] & find him in good health. I hear the
book about him has appeared[5]—but I shan't read it.[6]—

Write to me again before long! *Good luck!*

Affectionately

Ludwig Wittgenstein

[1] While working as a porter at Guy's Hospital Wittgenstein had been invited
to have his meals in the Doctors' Mess. There he became acquainted with Dr. R. T.
Grant, who was investigating the physiology of 'shock'. Dr. Grant found Wittgenstein's questions and suggestions about this investigation so relevant that he
invited him to join his research team when it moved to the Royal Victoria
Infirmary in Newcastle. Drury visited Wittgenstein there in 1943. Dr. Grant had
asked Wittgenstein to study the relationship between breathing and pulse. Wittgenstein took Drury to the laboratory and showed him the apparatus that he had
himself designed. Wittgenstein acted as his own subject, obtaining the necessary
tracings on a revolving drum. Dr. Grant was so impressed by Wittgenstein's
work that, according to Drury, he said he 'wished Wittgenstein had been a phy-
siologist and not a philosopher' (Drury in Rhees, op. cit., p. 147).

[2] I had been transferred to a destroyer-escort and expected to be on Atlantic
convoy duty. I had said in a letter to Wittgenstein that I might some day be able
to pay him a brief visit if my ship came to England.

[3] Rush Rhees, a student and close friend of Wittgenstein, and also a friend of
mine. He was Senior Lecturer in Philosophy at the University College of Swansea, and is one of the executors and editors of Wittgenstein's literary estate.

[4] Moore came to the USA as a Visiting Professor at Smith College in the Fall
Semester of 1940. He held the same appointment at Princeton in the Spring
Semester of 1941 while I was still at Princeton, and so I did see him frequently.

[5] *The Philosophy of G. E. Moore* in The Library of Living Philosophers, edited
by P. A. Schilpp, (Northwestern University, Chicago, 1942). This book consists
of articles by a number of philosophers, about various aspects of Moore's philosophical work, together with Moore's replies to those articles, and also Moore's
'An Autobiography'.

[6] Wittgenstein strongly disapproved of Moore's agreeing to the production of
such a book.

8   Clinical Research Lab.
                                         Royal Victoria Infirmary
                                         Newcastle
                                         7.12.43.

Dear Malcolm,

I haven't heard from you for ages. I'm still at my old work but
may possibly leave here soon as my boss is going into the army &
the whole research unit may brake up, or get another boss. I am
feeling rather lonely here & may try to get to some place where I
have someone to talk to. E.g. to Swansea where Rhees is a lecturer
in philosophy. I don't know if you remember Rhees. You saw him
in my lectures I believe. He was a pupil of Moore's & is an excellent man & has a real talent for philosophy, too. I haven't seen
Smythies for ages, nor heard from him, but someone told me that
he has a job at Oxford. (Not at the University.). I'm in good health
but often depressed.—If you feel like writing to me I'ld like to hear
from you; but if you don't feel like writing—don't.

                                  Good luck!
                                  Affectionately
                                  Ludwig Wittgenstein

9   Trinity College
                                         Cambridge
                                         16.11.44.

My dear Malcolm,

Thanks for your letter, dated Nov. 12th, which arrived this
morning. I was glad to get it. I thought you had almost forgotten
me, or perhaps wished to forget me. I had a particular reason for
thinking this. Whenever I thought of you I couldn't help thinking
of a particular incident[1] which seemed to me very important. You
& I were walking along the river towards the railway bridge & we
had a heated discussion in which you made a remark about
'national character' that shocked me by it's primitiveness. I then
thought: what is the use of studying philosophy if all that it does
for you is to enable you to talk with some plausibility about some
abstruse questions of logic, etc., & if it does not improve your
thinking about the important questions of everyday life, if it does
not make you more conscientious than any . . . journalist in the
use of the DANGEROUS phrases such people use for their own ends.
You see, I know that it's difficult to think *well* about 'certainty',

'probability', 'perception', etc. But it is, if possible, still more difficult to think, or *try* to think, really honestly about your life &
other peoples lives. And the trouble is that thinking about these
things is *not thrilling*, but often downright nasty. And when it's
nasty then it's *most* important.—Let me stop preaching. What I
wanted to say was this: I'ld *very* much like to see you again; but if
we meet it would be wrong to avoid talking about serious non-philosophical things. Being timid I don't like clashes, & particularly
not with people I like. But I'ld rather have a clash than mere superficial talk.—Well, I thought that when you gradually ceased writing to me it was because you felt that if we were to dig down deep
enough we wouldn't be able to see eye to eye in very serious matters. *Perhaps I was quite wrong.* But anyway, if we live to see each
other again let's not shirk digging. You can't think decently if you
don't want to hurt yourself. I know all about it because I am a
shirker.

I haven't seen Smythies for a *long* time, but shall see him in
about 2 weeks when he'll come up from Oxford (where he has a
job, not connected with the University) to read a paper to the Moral
Science Club.—Read this letter in good spirit! *Good luck!*

Affectionately
Ludwig Wittgenstein

[1] This incident occurred in the autumn of 1939 and is described in my
Memoir (p. 30).

10   Trinity College
Cambridge
22.5.45.

My dear Malcolm,

This morning I had your last letter from Brooklyn.[1] Had I had it
before I saw you it would have made getting into contact with you
rather easier. I worked (dictated) till one o.c. & then remembered
that I might still go to the station & see you off. I looked at a time-
table & saw that there was a good train to London at exactly 1 o.c.
& no good train after that for some time. So I concluded you were
taking the 1 o.c. train & that I'ld be too late. Later Wisdom told me
you had gone by a 1:50 train—which I could still have caught. I was
sorry I didn't try for that one. I should have liked to have told you
about getting your letter & and also to have repeated that I was glad
to have seen you. I imagine there was a lot on *your* mind as well as

on mine when you were with me. If you write to me, as I hope you will, you might call me by my Christian name & let me do the same. In case this should seem silly, or somehow wrong, to you, just say so frankly. I shan't be hurt.

Good luck! Affectionately
Ludwig Wittgenstein

[1] In May 1945 my ship came into Southampton with a convoy. I obtained a brief leave to visit Cambridge. The meeting with Wittgenstein, described in my Memoir (p. 36), was grim. The day after the meeting with Wittgenstein he received a letter from me, posted some weeks before, which was in response to his Letter 9.

I I   Trinity College
Cambridge
26.6.45

Dear Norman,

It was good to get your letter of June 21st. I want to say something about the war being a 'boredom'. If a boy said that school was an intensive boredom one might answer him that, if he only could get himself to learn what can really be learned there, he would not find it *so* boring. Now forgive me for saying that I can't help believing that an enormous lot can be learnt about human beings in this war—*if* you can keep your eyes open. And the better you are at thinking the more you'll get out of what you see. For thinking is *digesting*. If I'm writing in a preaching tone I'm just an ass! but the fact remains that if you're bored a lot it means that your mental digestion isn't what it should be. I think a good remedy for this is sometimes opening your eyes wider. Sometimes a book helps a little, e.g. T's 'Hadshi Murat'[1] wouldn't be bad. If you can't get it in America let me know. I *might* be able to get it here. I've tried the various booksellers in Cambridge but they haven't got it & say they can't get it. Smythies said one might get it at the Oxford University Press.

My work is going damn slowly. I wish I could get a volume ready for publishing by next autumn; but I probably shan't. I'm a *bloody* bad worker!

I'm looking forward to the magazines! It was *very* nice of you to send them.

There is another fair in Cambridge now, much bigger than the one we went to. I rolled a few pennies[2] but didn't win a thing! I need *you*.

Smythies was glad to see you. He sends his good wishes.—So do I! Look after yourself, body & soul, & be good all round!

So long!

Affectionately

Ludwig Wittgenstein

[1] Tolstoy's *Hadji Murat*, which Wittgenstein did send to me.
[2] Wittgenstein liked fairs and loved to roll pennies for prizes (Memoir, p. 45).

12

c/o Rhees
96 Bryn Rd.
Swansea
17.8.45.

Dear Norman,

Today I had your parcel with the detective mags. Thanks a lot! They're the real thing! As you see I'm in Wales. I got here a few days ago & should like to stay all through September. I enjoy the climate & *not* being in Cambridge.

Rhees, whom I think you remember, is here & I see a good deal of him.—We've had two VJ days[1] & I think there was much more noise than real joy.—I've been working a good deal this last academic year, I mean for myself & *if* everything goes well I might publish by Christmas. Not that what I've produced is good, but it is now about as good as I can make it. I think when it'll be finished I ought to come into the open with it. (By the way, this isn't gossip.)—I hope you're quite safe by now & that you'll be plain Mr., or Dr., soon. Also hope to see you before long & to tell you all I think of you. Rhees sends his best wishes. And so do I. Look after yourself externally & internally. So long!

Thanks again!

Affectionately

Ludwig Wittgenstein

[1] Victory in Europe and Victory in Asia.

13

c/o Rhees
96 Bryn Rd.
Swansea
S. Wales
[no date][1]

Dear Norman,

Thanks for your letter of Aug. 12th. Yes, I think I understand why a ship isn't a good place for 'thinking'[2]—I mean, *apart* from the fact that you're very busy. Perhaps I ought to feel elated because the war is over. But I'm not. I can't help feeling certain that this peace is only a truce. And the pretence that the complete stamping out of the 'aggressors' of this war will make this world a better place to live in, as a future war could, of course, only be started by them, stinks to high heaven &, in fact, promises a horrid future.

After these cheering thoughts let me tell you that I'm having a fairly good holiday here & that I'm feeling pretty stupid. Perhaps you'll say you've gathered as much from this letter already.—Rhees sends you his kind regards.—I hope you'll soon be demobilized & that then we'll be able to have talks, not just writes. I'm glad you got 'Hadshi Murat' & I hope you'll get a lot out of it, because there is a lot *in* it. I don't know any of the German books you mention but I'm suspicious about them—because of their authors & for other reasons.—As I said: I hope you'll enjoy the Tolstoy. There's a REAL man; who has a *right* to write.

I had your mags 3 or 4 days ago & immediately thanked you for them in a letter which I hope you'll receive soon. They're really grand.

> So long! Good luck!
> Affectionately
> Ludwig

[1] This undated letter was probably written in August 1945.
[2] In response to Letter 11 I had probably written to him that life on a crowded war vessel was not conducive to quiet thinking.

14

c/o Rhees
96 Bryn Rd.
Swansea
8.9.45

Dear Norman,

You're terrific!—Thanks a lot for the mags. It's nice getting a parcel from you, not only because of its contents.

The one way in which the ending of Lend-Lease really hits me is by producing a shortage of detective mags in this country. I can only hope Lord Keynes will make this quite clear in Washington. For I say: if the U.S.A. won't give us detective mags we can't give them philosophy, & so America will be the loser in the end. See?— I'm still in Swansea & enjoying my absence from Cambridge. My work isn't going well; partly because I've contracted some trouble with one of my kidneys. Nothing serious, but it makes me jumpy

& bad tempered. (I've always got some excuse.)—The other day I read Johnson's 'Life of Pope' & liked it very much. As soon as I get to Cambridge I'm going to send you a little book 'Prayers & Meditations' by Johnson. You may not like it at all,—on the other hand you may. I do.

This is all for now. Most of this page & the next page I will leave free in case you want to make any notes. I *hope* to see you before very long! Good luck! Thanks again!

Affectionately
Ludwig

15
c/o Rhees
96 Bryn Rd.
Swansea
20.9.45.

Dear Norman,

Thanks for your letter of Sept 9th. I'm glad to hear that you're going to get out of the Navy before long & I hope you'll come to Cambridge before I make up my mind to resign the absurd job of a prof. of philosophy. It is a kind of living death.—I'm going back to it in a fortnight.—I once tried to read 'Resurrection' but couldn't.[1] You see, when Tolstoy just tells a story he impresses me infinitely more than when he addresses the reader. When he turns his back to the reader then he seems to me *most* impressive. Perhaps one day we can talk about this. It seems to me his philosophy is most true when its *latent* in the story. Talking of philosophy: my book is gradually nearing its final form, & if you're a good boy & come to Cambridge I'll let you read it. It'll probably disappoint you. And the truth is: it's pretty lousy. (Not that I could improve on it essentially if I tried for another 100 years.) This, however, doesn't worry me. What I hear about Germany & Austria does. The re-educators of the Germans are doing nicely. Pity there won't be many left to enjoy the fruit of re-education.

My landlord has a modern American translation of the Bible. I dislike the translation of the N.T. (by a man E. J. Goodspeed) but the translation of the O.T. (by a group of people) makes a lot of things clearer to me & seems to me *well* worth reading. Perhaps you'll see it one day.

So long! Look after yourself!
Affectionately
Ludwig

[1] Tolstoy's *Resurrection*: I had been struck by a passage in this novel and had quoted it in the letter to which Wittgenstein was replying. The passage is the following, although the translation differs somewhat from the one I read in 1945:

> One of the commonest and most generally accepted delusions is that every man can be qualified in some particular way—said to be kind, wicked, stupid, energetic, apathetic and so on. People are not like that. We may say of a man that he is more often kind than cruel, more often wise than stupid, more often energetic than apathetic or vice versa; but it could never be true to say of one man that he is kind or wise, and of another that he is wicked or stupid. Yet we are always classifying mankind in this way. And it is wrong. Human beings are like rivers: the water is one and the same in all of them but every river is narrow in some places, flows swifter in others; here it is broad, there still, or clear, or cold, or muddy or warm. It is the same with men. Every man bears within him the germs of every human quality, and now manifests one, now another, and frequently is quite unlike himself, while still remaining the same man. (Tolstoy, *Resurrection*, Part I, Ch. 59, translated by Rosemary Edmonds: Penguin Classic, 1966.)

16   Trinity College
Cambridge
6.10.45.

Dear Norman,

This is the little book[1] I promised to send you. It seems to be out of print so I'm sending you my own copy. I wish to say that normally I can't read any printed prayers but that Johnson's impressed me by being *human*. Perhaps you'll see what I mean if you read them. As likely as not you won't like them *at all*. Because you will probably not look at them from the *angle* from which I see them. (But you might.) If you don't like the book throw it away. Only first cut out the leaf with my dedication. For when I shall become *very* famous it'll become very valuable as an autograph, & your grandchildren may be able to sell it for a lot of 'dough'.—I'm back in Cambridge & feeling pretty lousy. God knows what my lectures will be like! Wish me luck!—I wish you lots of luck, too. Smythies sends you his best wishes.

Let me hear from you before long.

Affectionately
Ludwig

[1] Samuel Johnson, *Prayers & Meditations*, 3rd ed. (H. R. Allenson, London): no date, but apparently 1826 or 1827 (1st ed. 1785).

17   Trinity College
                                                Cambridge
                                                30.10.45.

Dear Norman,

Thanks for your letter of Oct. 23rd. I'm glad you had a good holiday & glad that you plan coming here next year. Well, I'll try to be
here then. My job is a very, very dubious one for a dozen different
reasons.—My class just now is fairly large, 19 people. Many of
them will drop off, of course, & I wish this process could be acceler-
ated.—Smythies is coming & a woman who's very good, i.e., *more*
than just *intelligent*. There is also an Indian (or, at least, he is dark)
who seems to be all right; also two American soldiers: one's a dud,
the other's nice but I don't think he knows what we're talking
about.—If you'll read my book you'll have to read German. May be
if I find a nice German book I'll send it to you to brush up your German.—I see Moore about once every 3 weeks. He's in very good
health. Smythies is very overworked & looks pale & very thin, I'm
sorry to say.

Be good! & think decent & intelligent thoughts. And not just
about logic & philosophy, etc!

I'm looking forward very much to the mental nourishment
you've promised me. If I read your mags I often wonder how anyone
can read 'Mind'[1] with all its impotence & bankruptcy when they
could read Street & Smyth mags. Well, everyone to his taste.—
Good luck!

                                                Affectionately
                                                Ludwig

[1] *Mind* was and is a leading philosophical journal, published in England.

18   Trinity College
                                                Cambridge
                                                6.12.45.

Dear Norman,

Thanks for your letter & thanks for sending me van Houten's
cocoa. I'm looking forward to drinking it.—I, too, was greatly
impressed when I first read Freud.[1] He's extraordinary.—Of course
he is full of fishy thinking & his charm & the charm of the subject
is so great that you may easily be fooled.

He always stresses what great forces in the mind, what strong prejudices work against the idea of psycho-analysis. But he never says what an enormous charm that idea has for people, just as it has for Freud himself. There may be strong prejudices against uncovering something nasty, but sometimes it is infinitely more *attractive* than it is repulsive. Unless you think *very* clearly psycho-analysis is a dangerous & a foul practice, & it's done no end of harm &, comparatively, very little good. (If you think I'm an old spinster— think again!)—All this, of course, doesn't detract from Freud's extraordinary scientific achievement. Only, extraordinary scientific achievements have a way, these days, of being used for the destruction of human beings. (I mean their bodies, or their souls, *or their intelligence*). *So hold on to your brains.*

The painting of the enclosed Xmas card has given me great trouble. The thick book is my collected works.[2]

Smythies sends his best wishes.

Lots of good luck! May we see each other again!

Affectionately
Ludwig

[1] I had begun to read Freud and had told Wittgenstein in a letter that I was greatly impressed by him.

[2] Wittgenstein always bought extremely florid Xmas and Easter cards: they had to be 'soupy'. The card he enclosed with this letter included a 'painting' of a thick book.

19   c/o Rev. Morgan
                                   Cwmdoukin Terrace
                                   Swansea
                                   15.12.45.

Dear Norman,

Thanks for the detective mags! They are *rich* in mental vitamins & calories. It was nice getting them from you & also your Xmas card!

I'm in Swansea again over Christmas & probably over New Year. The weather's foul, but I enjoy not being in Cambridge. I know quite a number of people here whom I like. I seem to find it more easy to get along with them here than in England. I feel much more often like smiling, e.g. when I walk in the street, or when I see children, etc. Just now I feel *very* stupid. I ought to do some work but I don't. Last term my lectures didn't go too bad, on the whole. At the beginning of the term I thought I wouldn't be able to manage them. I felt a queer kind of exhaustion, sometimes coming on suddenly.

Then a doctor prescribed me glucose & that helped me enormously & I was pretty fit afterwards.

I'll stop now. This letter's lousy, I know. But it's as good as I can do just now.

Good luck! Be good!
Affectionately
Ludwig

20   Trinity College
                                                           Cambridge
                                                           15.1.46

Dear Norman,

Your parcel containing cocoa & peaches arrived today. Thanks ever so much. It was lovely to get it. And is the cocoa good!!—I've had almost a month in Swansea & I haven't done a stroke of work. I wish all your food for my body & mind could go to a better person. My lectures begin in 3 days. I'll talk a lot of rubbish. It would be nice if you could come to Cambridge[1] for an academic year before I resign my job! It might be a good thing, & a good conclusion for my dubious professorial career.

Thanks again! & let me know how you're getting on.

Affectionately
Ludwig

[1] I was released from the Navy in the autumn of 1945, and was reappointed as an Instructor at Princeton for the spring term of 1946. I had written to Wittgenstein that I wanted to spend the academic year 1946–7 in Cambridge and had applied for a Guggenheim Fellowship for that purpose.

21   Trinity College
                                                           Cambridge
                                                           25.4.46.

My dear Norman,

Thank you ever so much for the mags I got from you yesterday. It was good to feel that we are still in contact. I feel *very* perturbed in my mind. I haven't done any decent work for ages apart from my classes. They went all right last term. But now my brain feels burnt out, as though only the four walls were left standing, & some charred remains! Let's hope that I'll be in moderately good condition when you'll be here! I'm looking forward to seeing you.[1] I spent most of the Easter vac in Swansea. I saw Rhees there & had discussions with him. I came up the day before yesterday. I haven't yet seen Smythies. Tomorrow's my first lecture. *Oh hell!!*

I wish you a better head & a better heart than I have.

Affectionately
Ludwig

[1] I had written to Wittgenstein that I had been awarded the Fellowship and would definitely be coming to Cambridge.

22

Trinity College
Cambridge
27.8.47.[1]

Dear Norman,

Thanks for your letter which I received about 3 weeks ago. You know how much I enjoyed being with you at Cambridge. And, of course, you owe me *nothing*.[2] My mind is rather in a turmoil these days. I am almost certain that I shall resign my professorship in the autumn. I have not yet told Rollins, & *please keep it to yourself* as it's not yet certain. I *hate* to let down Rollins[3] & ——, but I think I won't be able to help it. I'ld like to be alone somewhere & try to write & to make at least one part of my book publishable. I'll never be able to do it while I'm teaching at Cambridge. Also I think that, quite apart from writing, I need a longish spell of thinking *alone*, without having to talk to anybody. But I haven't yet told the authorities about my plan & I don't intend to do so until October when I'll decide definitely.

I wish you *all possible good luck* & I hope that I shall see you again one day! It was good to be with you! Give my warmest wishes to Lee & my 'good luck' to Ray.

Let me hear from you!

Affectionately
Ludwig

P.S. I'm going to Austria on Sept 10th until about Oct 7th. Trinity will always find me.

[1] There was an interval of 16 months between this letter and the previous one. I had arrived in Cambridge in August 1946, accompanied by my wife, Leonida (Lee), and our son, Raymond (Ray). In the Summer of 1947 we returned to the USA, where I took up an appointment as an Assistant-Professor of Philosophy at Cornell University, Ithaca, N.Y.

[2] Soon after my return to the US I had written to Wittgenstein, expressing my gratitude to him for sharing his thoughts with me.

[3] Calvin Rollins, an American acquaintance of mine, had hoped to attend

Wittgenstein's lectures in the autumn of 1947. Rollins was later a Professor of
Philosophy in universities in Australia, Canada, and the USA.

23   Trinity College
                                                Cambridge
                                                16.11.47.

My dear Norman,

As soon as I returned here from Austria I tendered my resignation to the Vice Chancellor & I shall cease to be professor on Dec.
31st. at 12 p.m. *Whatever* happens to me (& I'm not at all sanguine
about my future) I feel I did the only natural thing. I intend to leave
here for Ireland in about 3 weeks. I don't know what my address
will be, but 'Trinity Coll. Cambridge' will always find me. I'm *very*
busy these days; chiefly, dictating stuff I wrote during the last 2–3
years. It's mostly *bad* but I want to have it with me in a handy
form.—I'm seeing Moore once a week. I like being with him almost
more than ever. Somehow we seem to understand each other
better. He is alternately well & a little ill & has to take it easy.

I'll write more some time soon. Just now I'm always in a hurry.
Give my warmest wishes to Lee & Raymond. GOOD LUCK!

                                                Affectionately
                                                Ludwig

I had an impertinent letter[1] from —— reproaching me for not letting him know beforehand about my resignation. He told me that
this showed a 'shocking' 'fault of character' & that I was 'a gross
person'. I replied & tried to tell him 'where he gets off'. He *seems* to
be an ass.

                        So long! Let me hear from you before long!
                                                The above.

[1] I refer to this incident in the Memoir (pp. 53–4).

24   c/o Mrs Kingston
                                                Kilpatrick House
                                                Red Cross
                                                Wicklow
                                                Eire
                                                9.12.47.

Dear Norman,

Thank you for two letters, or rather a letter & a Xmas card. I was
very pleased to get them. I have only today moved into the above

address. It's a little Guest House 2½ to 3 hours by bus from Dublin. It's not *too* bad & I hope I'll acclimatize. I'm the only guest. Of course, right now I still feel completely strange & uncomfortable. It's been pretty cold the last fortnight & looking for a place was very depressing. That I haven't worked a stroke for ages goes without saying. I'm looking forward to receiving the det. mags & the book. I, too, have sent you a very small present. I don't mean that *yours* is small. I hope you'll get it.—The idea of staying with you & Lee[1] some day appeals to me very much. I have *plenty* of money, though. If I were as rich in other respects I'd be *very* happy!

It was very kind of Lee to write to me on the Xmas card. Give her & Ray all my best wishes. I wish you lots of luck & know you wish me the same. Both of us need it like Hell. *

Affectionately
Ludwig

* And other people do too.

[1] We had suggested to Wittgenstein that he might like to visit us in our home in Ithaca.

25   Kilpatrick House
                                                Red Cross
                                                Wicklow
                                                Eire
                                                4.1.48.

Dear Lee,

Thank you for your very nice letter. I'm a *much* worse correspondent than you are. I spent Christmas alone here, but on Boxing Day I saw two friends, one of whom had come over from England to see me & stayed with me here for a few days.—This is a pretty quiet place, & if it were still more quiet it would suit me *still* better. My work's going moderately well & I think it might even go very well if I weren't suffering from some kind of indigestion which I don't seem to be able to shake off. I'll have to come to Ithaca & eat your good cooking.—Actually its gradually getting better, & my landlady here gives me all I need.—I was a bit worried by what you write me about Norman, that he's working so d . . . hard. Please tell him from me not to overdo it. I seriously admire his energy; but a man can only do *so much.*—Your lovely present has arrived. Thanks a lot! I'll now have enough to read for a whole year.

I think it's a *very* good idea to make Ray read to you. To practice reading aloud *well*, i.e. carefully, teaches one *a lot*! E.g. how rotten & slapdash most people, & the newspapers, write; & they write as they *think*. I'm sure horses won't be bad company for Ray.

I heard from Shah & Kreisel & Hijab & Hunt. Shah & a few other students are having regular discussions in Shah's room, &, apparently they aren't too bad, & some of the Moral Science Club meetings at which no dons are present are tolerable, too.

I very much hope that some day I'll be able to be with you again & to have talks with Norman.

My love to all of you! & thanks again.

Ludwig

P.S. I've never heard of Rosenthal,[1] which means nothing.

---

[1] I believe that in a letter I had made a reference to my friend, Thomas Rosenmeyer, whom Wittgenstein had briefly encountered in Cambridge (Memoir, p. 31). I suspect that 'Rosenthal' is Rosenmeyer. Rosenmeyer became a Professor of Classics at the University of California, Berkeley.

26
Kilpatrick House
Red Cross
Wicklow
Eire
5.2.48.

Dear Norman,

I had your letter of Jan. 6th a good long time ago. Thanks! I am now in very good bodily health & my work isn't going bad either. I have occasionally queer states of nervous instability about which I'll only say that they're rotten while they last, & teach one to pray.

I've never read 'The works of love'.[1] Kierkegaard is far too deep for me, anyhow. He bewilders me without working the good effects which he would in *deeper* souls.—Years ago Drury read to Skinner & me the beginning of the 'Conquest of Mexico'[2] which we found very interesting indeed. That I didn't like the parsonish point of view of Prescott's is, of course, a different story.—I am not reading much, thank God. I read in Grimm's fairy tales & in Bismarck's 'Gedanken & Erinnerungen' [Thoughts and reminiscences] which I admire greatly. I don't mean, of course, that my views are Bismarck's views. It's written in very excellent, though rather difficult German, as the sentences are very long. Otherwise I'd recommend you to look at it.

I wish you *lots* of good luck, & I know you wish me the same; & *do I need it!*

All the best to Lee & Ray.
Affectionately
Ludwig

I haven't anyone at all to talk to here, & this is good & in a way bad. It would be good to see someone occasionally to whom one could say a really friendly word. I don't need *conversations.* What I'd like would be someone to smile at occasionally.

[1] I was reading Kierkegaard's *The Works of Love,* translated from the Danish by D. F. and L. M. Swenson (Princeton University Press, Princeton, 1946). I was greatly impressed by it and had said so in a letter.

[2] In the same letter I spoke of enjoying W. H. Prescott's *History of the Conquest of Mexico* (3 vols., London, 1843).

27   Kilpatrick House
                                         Red Cross
                                         Wicklow
                                         Eire
                                         15.3.48.

Dear Norman,

Thanks for your letter which I got a few weeks ago. v. Wright[1] wrote to me about his putting in for the professorship & asked me to write him a recommendation. I did, & it won't be the recommendation's fault if he doesn't get the job. I don't know *at all* what his chances are. I'm *slightly* doubtful because of his being another foreigner.—My work is progressing *very* slowly & painfully, but it is progressing. I wish I had more working power & didn't tire so *very* easily. But I have to take it as I find it—Your mags are wonderful. How people can read Mind if they could read Street & Smith beats me. If philosophy has anything to do with wisdom there's certainly not a grain of that in Mind, & quite often a grain in the detective stories.

That'll be all for today because my brain feels very stuffy indeed.

Good wishes!
Affectionately
Ludwig

[1] Georg Henrik von Wright was then a Professor of Philosophy in Finland. He attended Wittgenstein's lectures in 1939 and in 1947 and they became friends. He was elected to succeed Wittgenstein as Professor of Philosophy at Cambridge. After a few years he resigned in order to return to Finland. He is a Member of the Academy of Finland and is an Honorary Fellow of Trinity College,

Cambridge. He is one of the executors and editors of Wittgenstein's literary estate. He and I first became acquainted when we were both attending Wittgenstein's lectures in 1947, and we have maintained a continuous personal and professional friendship ever since.

28

Rosro Cottage
Renvyle P.O.
Co Galway
Eire
30.4.48.

Dear Norman,

This is chiefly to give you my new address. I've had a bad time lately: soul, mind & body. I felt exceedingly depressed for many weeks, then fell ill & now I'm weak & completely dull. I haven't done any work for 5–6 weeks. I'm living alone in a cottage here on the west coast right on the sea, far from civilization. I arrived here 2 days ago & am not yet at home at all. I'll have to learn gradually how to do my housework without losing too much time & strength. During my illness I read 'Monkey'[1] &, to my surprise, found it agreeable to read, I hadn't expected it.—What gets me down most is that my nights are bad. If they mend, & I hope they will, I have a chance.—I haven't heard from Smythies or Miss Anscombe[2] for a *long* time. I had a letter from von Wright a few days ago. He had lots of anxiety recently for political reasons, but things seem to be less dangerous now.—Do you ever hear from Moore? I shan't write more today, I'm much too dull. Give my best wishes to Lee & Ray & look after yourself!

Affectionately
Ludwig

[1] I had sent Wittgenstein a copy of the sixteenth-century Chinese folk novel *Monkey*, by Wu Ch'Eng-en, translation from the Chinese by Arthur Waley (Grove Press, New York, 1943).

[2] G. E. M. Anscombe, a student and friend of Wittgenstein. She became a Lecturer in Philosophy and a Fellow of Somerville College, Oxford; later Professor of Philosophy at Cambridge. She is one of the executors and editors of Wittgenstein's writings, and is the principal translator of those writings from German to English. I first met her and her husband, Peter Geach, in Cambridge in 1946, and we have been friends since that time.

29

Rosro Cottage
Renvyle P.O.
Co Galway
Eire
4.6.48.

Dear Norman,

Thanks a lot for the detective mags. I had, before they arrived, been reading a detective story by Dorothy Sayers, & it was so bl . . . foul that it depressed me. Then when I opened one of your mags it was like getting out of a stuffy room into the fresh air. And, talking of detective fiction, I'd like you to make an enquiry for me when once you've got nothing better to do. A couple of years ago I read with great pleasure a detective story called 'Rendezvous with fear' by a man Norbert Davis.[1] I enjoyed it so much that I gave it not only to Smythies but also to Moore to read & both shared my high opinion of it. For, though, as you know, I've read hundreds of stories that *amused* me & that I liked reading, I think I've only read two perhaps that I'd call *good stuff*, & Davis's is one of them. Some weeks ago I found it again by a queer coincidence in a village in Ireland, it has appeared in an edition called 'Cherry Tree books', something like 'Penguin'.—Now I'd like you to ask at a bookshop if Norbert Davis has written other books, & what kind. (He's an American) It may sound crazy, but when I recently re-read the story I liked it again so much that I thought I'd really like to write to the author & thank him. If this is nuts don't be surprised, for so am I.—I shouldn't be surprised if he had written quite a lot & only this one story were really good.

My work's so-so; not too good, not *too* bad. I don't think I'd be much good at philosophical discussion now; but this may mend & then I hope I'll have talks with you!—May you be lucky in every way! Give my good wishes to L. & R.[2]

Affectionately
Ludwig

L & R are usually called 'liquida'.

[1] As I recall, I was unable to obtain any information about this author.
[2] Lee and Ray.

30

Rosro Cottage
Renvyle P.O.
Co Galway
Eire
5.6.48.

Dear Lee,

I discovered your kind letter this morning & might not have seen it for a long time if I hadn't opened this particular detective mag. Thanks *a lot* for inviting me. It's good to know that you won't mind taking me in once the time is ripe. But it isn't now. You see, my main source of trouble is myself &, unfortunately, that would accompany me wherever I go. I'm *much* better now than before I came here. My health is as fine as can be expected of an old codger, & the things that I'm always inclined to beef about are *necessary* evils. My work, e.g., is only so-so; but then my talent is only *that* size & I'm getting a bit shop worn & nothing can help this. I often get exasperated about it but I just must (or *ought to*) learn to bear it. The solitude here is often a strain, but it's also a blessing; that I have to do all my housework is a great strain, but it's undoubtedly a great blessing, too, because it keeps me sane, it *forces* me to live a regular life & is in general good for me *although I curse it every day*. The truth is I oughtn't to be so much an old woman & complain such a lot; but then that's also one of the things that can't be changed.—But I hope, *seriously*, to come & stay with you one day when I'll be riper for it. (Of course you know that some apples never get ripe: they're hard & sour until they get soft & mushy.)— The country around here is pretty wild & I enjoy walking in it though I don't go for long walks. I like looking at the various sea birds; we have also seals, though I've only seen one so far. I see nobody except the man who brings me my milk every day. He also helps around the house a little & sees that I don't run out of turf (that's what we heat & cook with). He's quite nice & certainly better company than the people I stayed with in Co Wicklow. The nearest village is 10 miles away. When I want anything special in the way of groceries I write to Galway & they send it here by post.—I hope Fate will let me stay with you some day, & I'm sure I'll enjoy it hugely, I also hope that then I might be useful in discussion (now I'm too stale).

Affectionately
Ludwig

31   Rosro Cottage
                                                        Renvyle P.O.
                                                        Co Galway
                                                        Eire
                                                        [no date]

Dear Norman,

Thanks ever so much for your letter of May 9th. I hope that one
day I shall be able to come & stay with you, & it's good to know
that Lee & you will have me. Right now I must stay here & try to
do moderately decent work. God alone knows if I'll succeed. I'm
not a bit sanguine about it, but I still try & hope.—By the time this
letter reaches you you'll probably have heard that von Wright has
been elected Professor at Cambridge.—It's extraordinary that you
can read the 'Häsichenbraut',[1] & not at all surprising that you find
some of the dialects unintelligible. After all, if an Austrian peasant
hears a North German speak he has the greatest difficulty to understand him, & if he heard a man speak in a Low German dialect (like
that of 'De Gaudeif un sien Meester') he wouldn't understand a
single word.—May your work go satisfactorily!!

Give my very best wishes to Lee & Raymond.

                                                As always, affectionately
                                                        Ludwig

There's one thing I'd be very grateful to you for sending me, i.e., a
tin or glass of some powdered coffee extract, like 'Nescafe', or one
made by a firm Borden. Lee will know what I mean. But do it only if
it's *very* easy for you.

[1] Wittgenstein sent me a two-volume edition of *Grimms Märchen* as a Christmas gift in 1946. In a letter I said that I had trouble with some of the dialects: I
could manage to read the story entitled 'Häsichenbraut' (The hare's bride), but
not the one entitled 'De Gaudeif un sien Meester' (The thief and his master).

32   Rosro Cottage
                                                        Renvyle P.O.
                                                        Co Galway
                                                        Eire
                                                        5.7.48.

Dear Norman,

I'm sure I have to thank both you & Lee for the marvelous parcel
which arrived 3 days ago. I ought to have known that if I ask you to
send anything (the Borden coffee) you'd send ten times more. It's

all lovely & most useful, but let it be my Christmas present, please.

My work isn't going well though it's moving a bit. The other day I asked myself: ought I to have left the University, oughtn't I to have gone on teaching after all? I immediately felt that I couldn't possibly have continued teaching philosophy & even told myself that perhaps I ought to have resigned sooner; but then I thought of you & v. Wright in Cambridge & said to myself that I'd left exactly at the right moment. If my philosophical talent comes to an end now it's bad luck, but that's all.

I intend to stay here another 3–4 weeks & then to go to Dublin to see Drury[1] for a few days, then to Oxford for a week or so, then I want to stay with Richards[2] (whom you haven't met) near London & after that I want to go to Austria for 3–4 weeks if I can get the permit. From Austria I'll return to this place, God being willing.— Do you remember Shah, the Indian who came to my classes? He came to Leeuane, a village 10 miles from here, & came to see me yesterday. I was glad to see him, although our talk wasn't particularly good (I'm often tired & irritable now, I'm *sorry* to say). He is leaving for India in August or September. He'd rather stay in Europe, I believe, but perhaps it'll be good for him to get out of this civilization for a bit. But how should *I* know!—Shah told me that Kreisel[3] *may* go to Princeton next year.

Thanks again & all good wishes to you & Lee! & Raymond.

Affectionately
Ludwig

[1] M. O'C. Drury, a student and long-time friend of Wittgenstein. Drury became a medical doctor and later a consultant in psychiatry in Dublin.

[2] Ben Richards, a student and friend of Wittgenstein, who became a medical doctor.

[3] George Kreisel, a mathematical logician who attended Wittgenstein's lectures. Later Kreisel held professorships in mathematical logic at a number of universities, including Stanford, Reading, and the Sorbonne.

33

Ross's Hotel
Parkgate Street
Dublin
6.11.48.

Dear Norman,

Thank you for your letter of Oct. 8th. I arrived here about 3 weeks ago after staying in Cambridge a fortnight & dictating some M.S.S. When I came here I found to my surprise that I could work again; & as I'm anxious to make hay during the very short period when the sun shines in my brain I've decided not to go to Rosro this winter but to stay here where I've got a warm & quiet room.

I'm seeing a good deal of two friends of mine, Drury & Richards, neither of whom you've met. I know that soon enough I'll have run dry again, but just now my mind feels alive.—In Cambridge I saw a good deal of Miss Anscombe & I had tea a couple of times with Rollins who didn't seem to me to have deteriorated. Which is something. I also saw Moore once. I liked being with him. I told him that you had written you hadn't heard from him, & he said he'd write to you soon. He was well when I saw him but he told me that he had not been well during the first part of the summer.

I should *like* you to have a typescript of my stuff but I don't see how I can let you have one at present. There exist only 3 copies. One I have (& I need it), Miss Anscombe has one, Moore has half, or $\frac{3}{4}$ of one & the remaining half or $\frac{1}{4}$ is somewhere among my things in Cambridge. There is no one here who could make another copy from mine, & it would cost a *lot* of money. Of course Miss Anscombe could send you her copy, but, to be quite honest, I'd rather it remained safely in England as long as there are only 3 copies existing. I hope you don't think me beastly. It's nice of you to want a copy of my stuff at all! I'll let you have one as soon as I can get another one made.

It's very kind of Lee to think of sending me some instant coffee. I'll be grateful for it, but SHE MUSTN'T SEND ANYTHING ELSE! I'm in good health & in much better spirits than I ought to be, being what I am.

Let me hope that I may see you again before very long!

Affectionately
Ludwig

P.S. I saw v. Wright in Cambridge, too, & had a few talks with him. I liked being with him. Give my best wishes to Lee & to Ray!

34

Ross's Hotel
Parkgate Street
Dublin
Eire
31.12.48.

Dear Lee,

Thank you & Norman ever so much for your wonderful present! As I've said before, you should be put under tutilage! And in that case I might try to get 'powers of attorney'. (That's the sort of thing I always read in my detective magazines.) Everything in the box was most useful & grand.—Some weeks ago I heard from Norman who wrote that he hadn't yet heard from Prof. Moore. I think by now he'll have got a letter from him.—You see, when I saw Moore 3 months ago I reminded him of *two* things, one of which was to write to Norman. So when I heard that he hadn't written to Norman I thought he might also have forgotten his second promise to me & I wrote him a letter with my Xmas card reminding him of *both*; to which I received an answer from him, saying that he'd done both things.—Rhees, whom you've met, is staying with me now for about a week. He is good company. I'm reading part of my stuff with him. When he leaves on Jan. 1st (tomorrow) I'll give him the tin of dried eggs from your parcel. I don't need it just now & he does. That reminds me: Your 'instant coffee' is lovely. I now see that Washington really was a great man.[1]—I had a Christmas card & a letter from Smythies. He seems to be well & working *hard*; I hope not *too* hard. I, too, am working a fair amount & still moderately well. I wish my luck could hold for another 6 months, for by then I could get a good chunk of work done.—The weather here is cold now, *far* too cold for my liking.—Thanks again, & thanks for the lovely card. All good wishes to you, Norman & Ray from

Ludwig

I often think of you & hope to see you all again before too long!
P.S. I had ordered for Norman a little book which, I thought, might interest him. Yesterday I found out from the *d* . . . . people in the bookshop that they hadn't given the publishers the right address! So heaven knows when it'll reach him! It's nothing anyhow, but I'm very sorry.

   I often think of you & hope to see you all again before too long!

[1] Presumably the name of the brand of instant coffee was 'Washington'.

35   Ross's Hotel
                                          Parkgate Street
                                          Dublin
                                          28.1.49.

Dear Norman,
   I'm really ashamed of asking the question which I'm writing to ask you.—Some time before Christmas I ordered a cheap little book

through a Dublin bookseller. The title is 'The Journals of George Fox' & it had appeared in Dent's 'Everyman's Library'. If it wasn't out of print, Dents in London were to send it straight to you (with a Xmas card from me). I thought you mightn't have it & that it might interest you.—Towards the end of December I called again at the book shop & was told that Dents had replied they couldn't send the book to America but that a firm, Dutton in New York, supplied America with the 'Everyman's Library'. I was told that they had already written to Dutton about it. By a mere chance I glanced in their order book & I saw that *all* the address they had put down was 'Dr. Malcolm, Ithaca, N.Y.'—I gave them a piece of my mind & again your full address, & they promised to write to Dutton immediately.—*Did you get the book?*[1]—I have no doubt, the card I gave the Dublin people was lost, so, even if you got the book, you couldn't have known who sent it.

I had a pretty good run of work in the last 3 months, or so, but I fell ill with some sort of infection of the intestines about 3 weeks ago & it hasn't yet cleared up. If it goes on for another week I shall consult a specialist. Of course it hasn't done my work any good. I had to interrupt it completely for a week & after that it just crawled along, as I do when I take a walk these days.

I hope you're all well, or moderately well. It would be good to see you again before long!

Give my good wishes to Lee & Raymond.

Affectionately
Ludwig

[1] Yes.

36

Ross's Hotel
Parkgate Street
Dublin
18.2.49.

Dear Norman,

Thanks for your letter. I'm glad you got the book. Somehow I'd been certain that they hadn't sent it to you.—But what a queer thing to write 'It's terribly nice of you to think of us'! You couldn't have thought at all when you wrote that.—Now as to Moore:[1]—I don't really understand Moore, &, therefore, what I'll say may be quite wrong. But this is what I'm inclined to say:—That Moore is in some sense extraordinarily childlike is obvious, & the remark you quoted (about vanity) is certainly an example of that childlikeness. There is also a *certain* innocence about Moore; he is, e.g., completely unvain. As to it's being to his *'credit'* to be childlike,—I can't understand that; unless it's also to a *child's* credit. For you aren't talking of the innocence a man has fought for, but of an innocence which comes from a natural absence of a temptation.—I believe that all you wanted to say was that you *liked*, or even *loved*, Moore's childlikeness. And that I can *understand*.—I think that our discrepancy here is not so much one of thoughts as of feelings. I *like* & greatly respect Moore, but that's all. He doesn't warm my heart (or very little), because what warms my heart most is human kindness, & Moore—*just like a child*—is not kind. He is kindly & he can be charming & nice to those he likes & he has great *depth*.—That's how it seems to me. If I'm wrong, I'm wrong.—My work is still going fairly well, though not as well as, say, 6 weeks ago. That's partly due to the fact that I've been a bit ill, & also that a number of things are really worrying me.—Money is not one of them. I am, of course, spending rather a lot, but I'll have enough for another 2 years, I think. During that time, God being willing, I'll get some work done; & that, after all, was why I resigned my professorship. I mustn't worry about money² now, for if I did I couldn't work. (What will happen after that time I don't yet know. Maybe I won't live that long anyway.)—One of my present worries is the health of one of my sisters in Vienna. She was operated on cancer a short time ago & the operation, as far as it went, was successful, but she won't have *long* to live. For that reason I *intend* to go to Vienna sometime next spring; & that's got something to do with you, because if I go & come back to England afterwards I intend to dictate the stuff that I've been writing since last autumn, & *if* I do, I'll send you a copy. May it act as manure on your field.

Give all my good wishes to Lee & Raymond. (I wish he'd *always* remain good-natured. But I know that's a tall order.) So long!

Affectionately
Ludwig

¹ In a letter to Wittgenstein I had related a conversation I had with Moore. We were speaking of an American philosopher of distinction, whom I knew. I said to Moore that this philosopher tended to be hostile to criticisms of his own philosophical writings. Moore looked puzzled. I said to him: 'Don't you understand how vanity might make a philosopher resent criticism of his work?' Moore took his pipe out of his mouth, shook his head, and said 'No!' In commenting on this incident to Wittgenstein I probably said that this was an example of Moore's

'innocence' and 'childlike' character, and that his being like that was a 'credit' to him.
[2] After resigning his professorship Wittgenstein had no income. I had expressed concern about whether he had enough money to live on. Upon his father's death in 1912 Wittgenstein inherited a large fortune. When he returned to Vienna after the war he immediately undertook to divest himself of his wealth. He gave it to his brothers and sisters. He once said: 'They have so much money already that some more won't do them any harm'! His sister, Hermine Wittgenstein, in her brief Memoir of Ludwig, relates that Ludwig's family and friends could not understand how he could want to give away *all* of his money *irrevocably*—with no provision for a sum being set aside in case he should later regret his decision. She says: 'A hundred times he wanted to assure himself that there was no possibility of any money still belonging to him in any shape or form. To the despair of the notary carrying out the transfer he returned to this point again and again' (Hermine Wittgenstein, 'My Brother Ludwig', in Rhees, op. cit., p. 4).

37   Ross's Hotel
                                               Parkgate Street
                                               Dublin
                                               19.3.49.

Dear Lee & Norman,

   Thank you ever so much for the kind invitation.[1] I got it almost a week ago but couldn't reply because my thoughts were in such a turmoil; & even today I may not be able to produce anything better than a jumble of incoherent sentences. First let me say a) that I feel deeply grateful for your kindness & b) that I feel *strongly* tempted to accept your invitation. But there are huge difficulties.—My eldest sister is, to the best of my knowledge, still alive & my two younger sisters *may* still want me to go to Vienna before long. If this happened I'd probably go to Vienna within the next 3 weeks & stay there for 3 or 4 weeks.—I went to a travel agency to enquire about going to America & found out that the journey there & back would cost me somewhere between 80 & 120 pounds. Further I'm told that you alone will have to pay for my upkeep in America, as I'm not allowed to take with me more than £5. In fact I gather that you'd have to send affidavits stating that you are able & willing to pay for all my expences during my stay in the U.S.A. If these regulations did not exist I could, theoretically, spend my own money in America, but in fact *I couldn't afford that*. I could afford the trip only by staying with you for 2 or 3 months & sponging on you!— Now the prospect of staying with you for that length of time is very pleasant as far as I'm concerned, but there is the snag that I am an elderly man & aging pretty rapidly. I mean, physically, not, as far as I can see, mentally. Now this means that you couldn't take me on any *tours*. I'm all right for strolling about but I can't do *very* much more than I did at Cambridge.—For the same reason I wouldn't be any good at gardening.—If it weren't for all these difficulties I'd come *like a shot*, for I'd love to stay with you, have discussions with one of you & make myself a general nuisance to the other.—I've forgotten another thing. If I booked a 3rd class passage right away I couldn't get a birth before the middle of July; if I booked 2nd class, which is *much* more expensive, I could travel towards the middle, or end of May. Heaven knows where you might be in July, but even if I came earlier I'd have to stay with you until September & be a dead weight during your summer vacations.—This, as far as I can see now in my confused state of mind, is the position.—

I imagine that you didn't quite realize all these snags when you invited me. Please take *everything* that I've said in this letter seriously & at it's face value.

Thank you again for your great kindness.

> Affectionately
> Ludwig

¹ In a letter to Wittgenstein we had definitely invited him to stay with us in the summer of 1949.

38   Ross's Hotel
                                          Parkgate Street
                                          Dublin
                                          1.4.49.

Dear Norman,

Thanks a lot for your letter of March 24th. I have booked a passage to New York on the Queen Mary July 21st, & if my health & other circumstances permit it I will come & be a d. . . . nuisance to you & Lee for 2 or 3 months. May everything go well.—I can't use your letter as an affidavit; it's a *much* more formal affair than you imagine. I enclose a cutting from the regulations & a form of affidavit. I know that all this red tape is hellish but we can't change it; so please read the damn thing through carefully & comply with all the requirements. There is one more thing I want to say: In this life one doesn't know what's going to happen; & so, supposing later on you were inclined, *for whatever reason*, to change your mind about the desirability of my visit, please *don't hesitate* to tell me so. I'm told that I can have *all* my money for the ticket refunded (except 10s, which is nothing).—I haven't been doing any work at all for the last 2–3 weeks. My mind is tired & stale, partly, I think because I'm a bit exhausted, partly because lots of things worry me terribly just now. I think I could still discuss philosophy if I had someone here to discuss with, but alone I can't concentrate on it. I suppose it'll all change some day. The sooner the better.—Well then, please send me that affidavit & prepare yourself for the shock of seeing me. I'm looking forward to seeing you & Lee & Ray again. Give my love to Lee.

Affectionately
Ludwig

39   Ross's Hotel
                                      Parkgate Street
                                      Dublin
                                      17.5.49.

My dear Norman,

Please forgive me for not writing sooner. I received your affidavit etc. about 3 weeks ago in Vienna. I went to Vienna in the middle of April to see my eldest sister who is very ill. When I left 5 days ago she was still alive but there is no hope of her recovering. I arrived here last night. While I was in Vienna I was hardly able to write at all. I felt so rotten myself. I haven't done any work since the beginning of March & I haven't had the strength of even *trying* to do any. God knows how things will go on now.—I shall go to the American Consulate here with your affidavit etc. & I'm sure it'll be all he wants if he isn't mad. As I think I've written to you, I have a ticket for the Queen Mary, sailing July 21st. I hope all of you are well, & I hope you won't find me a terribly disagreeable companion & bore when I come. All good wishes to all of you!

Affectionately
Ludwig

40   Ross's Hotel
                                      Parkgate Street
                                      Dublin
                                      4.6.49.

Dear Norman,

Thanks for your letter of May 30th. When I arrived here 3 weeks ago I went to see my doctor & he had my blood examined. They found that I had a severe anaemia of a rather unusual kind. It was

suspected that I had a growth in my stomach but the X-ray definitely showed that there is no such thing inside me. I'm being given
a lot of iron & liver extract & am getting better slowly. I think I
shall certainly be able to sail with the Queen Mary on July 21st.
There is, however, the question how far my anaemia will affect my
ability to discuss. At present I am quite unable to do any philosophy & I don't think I'd be strong enough to have even a moderately decent discussion. In fact at present I'm *sure* I couldn't do it.
But of course it's possible that by the end of July I may have recovered sufficiently for my brain to work again. I intend to go to
Cambridge in about 2 weeks & to dictate some stuff if I feel strong
enough. That will show me where I stand & I'll let you know the
result. Also I shall probably have a new blood examination done by
them & that'll also show something, in particular the rate at which
I'm progressing. I *know* that you'd extend your hospitality to me
even if I were *completely* dull & stupid, but *I* wouldn't want to be a
mere dead weight in your house. I want to feel that I can at least
give *a little* for so much kindness.—Anyhow, I hope that by July
21st I'll be a good deal more lively than now. (D. v.)—The American Counsul here has been pretty decent so far, but it turns out that
I shall have to get the visa from the London Consul because I
haven't resided in Ireland long enough. I hope that part of the matter will go moderately smoothly.—I know that Miss Anscombe &
Smythies have not forgotten you, but I understand that it's difficult
for them to write. I hardly ever hear from them, either.—I *very
much* look forward to seeing you! Give my love to Lee & Ray.

Affectionately
Ludwig

P.S. I'm getting a ticket from New York to Ithaca here, so it isn't
necessary that one of you should come & fetch me, but if it could
be done without difficulty I'd be very glad if you, or Lee did come to
meet me at New York as I'm such a complete stranger &
exceedingly clumsy these days.

41   Ross's Hotel
                                            Parkgate Street
                                            Dublin
                                            14.6.49.
Dear Norman,

Thanks for your very kind letter. I never meant to *pay* for your kindness in discussions. Anyhow, the best I could give you would be lousy payment. All I meant was: I don't want to bore my kind hosts to *death*. However, let's not talk about it any more, especially as I've got good news: I've improved greatly during the last few days. So, obviously, the iron & liver extract do work.—I'm *very* glad you've kept quiet about my visit & I *hope* —— will do the same. His proposal to drive us is most kind, there is, however, one thing I've got to say. I haven't seen —— for over 16 years, but when I knew him in Cambridge, though he seemed quite pleasant, I never thought highly of him as a serious thinker, & we never were particular *friends*. I'm saying this because I don't want him to believe that I'll be a *sociable* person. If you don't think that this misunderstanding might arise I'll be glad to accept his offer. I shan't cancel my ticket from New York to Ithaca; I'm told I can have it refunded completely if I don't use it, & one never knows. A ticket in the hand is better than two motor cars in the bush.—I didn't know how long the journey from New York to Ithaca was, & it would be *madness* for you &/or Lee to travel twice 8, or 9 hours to fetch me. So, if the car should be out of order, or off for any other reason, I'll jolly well travel to Ithaca alone. Maybe, like in the films, I'll find a beautiful girl whom I meet on the boat & who will help me. But, seriously, I'll be completely all right alone. When I wrote you the other day I was a bit funky because I wondered if my health would get better, but now I know that it is.—Just one more remark. Anything that I could be said ever to have done for you was either my duty (like lecturing), or was simply done because I enjoyed your company. Draw the conclusions yourself!—Yesterday I listened at the radio to part of a discussion between Prof. Ayer & a Jesuit[1] about Logical Positivism. I stood 40 minutes of it.

Give my love to Lee & to Ray.

Thanks for everything!   Affectionately
                                                Ludwig

[1] A. J. Ayer, Professor of Philosophy at Oxford. The Jesuit was Father Cople-stone. This was a discussion on the Third Programme. I believe that the topic was 'The Existence of God'.

42   40 Swakeley Rd
                                      Ickenham
                                      Uxbridge
                                      7.7.49.

Dear Norman,

Thanks for your letter of June 23rd. As to whether or not we should accept ——'s offer, I want *you* to decide. The only thing I'd like to say is, that *if* we accept, this should not entail that I must see a great deal of him once I'm in Ithaca. Whether there is such an entailment you'll be able to judge far better than I. If there is, I'd rather go by rail, but in that case it would be madness of you to come all the long way from Ithaca to fetch me. I already have a ticket to Ithaca (which I can get refunded in case I don't use it). Also I don't yet know what *time* the Queen Mary is supposed to arrive in New York, nor how far one can rely on the schedule. Supposing it arrived in the evening, could —— drive us back through the night, & wouldn't it be *very* disagreeable for him?—I'll wire you the time of arrival in a few days.—This letter is probably frightfully stupid, but I can't write a more helpful one. My anaemia is as good as cured, but unfortunately I'm still not the same I was before I got ill.—I'm looking forward immensely to seeing you & Lee, & I hope I shan't be too much trouble.

So long! & good luck!

                                      Affectionately
                                      Ludwig

P.S. *Whatever* you decide will be OK by me.[1]

[1] I decided to go to New York City by train to meet the ship. Wittgenstein and I returned to Ithaca the same day by train (Memoir, p. 68). This was in July 1949. Wittgenstein returned to England in October.

43   c/o Mrs. Rhees
                                      104 Goldhurst Terrace
                                      London N.W.6
                                      Monday [no date][1]

Dear Norman, Dear Lee,

You must have wondered why I didn't write to you for such a long time. Unfortunately I fell ill when I arrived here 10 days ago (some kind of flu). I'm better now, but still far from well. So, please forgive me if I don't write more than a few lines today. *Thanks for all your great kindness!* I wish I could have been a better guest.

I am staying with Mrs. Rhees,[2] who is very kind to me, until Wednesday. Then I'll probably go to Cambridge for a few days & after that to Dublin. Please send all my mail to Ross's Hotel, Parkgate Street, Dublin Eire.

Give my good wishes to Doney.[3]

Thanks again.

Affectionately
Ludwig

[1] The first letter from Wittgenstein after his return to England, probably written in November 1949.

[2] Jean Rhees, wife of Rush Rhees, and a Jungian psychoanalyst.

[3] Willis Doney, a friend of mine and an Instructor in Philosophy at Cornell; later a Professor of Philosophy at Dartmouth College. Doney took Wittgenstein for drives in his car and also participated in some of the philosophical discussions with Wittgenstein in Ithaca.

44

c/o v. Wright
'Strathaird'
Lady Margaret Rd
Cambridge
[no date][1]

Dear Norman,

Thanks for your letter! The doctors have now made their diagnosis. I have cancer of the prostate. But this sounds, in a way, much worse than it is, for there is a drug (actually some hormones) which can, as I'm told, alleviate the symptoms of the disease, so that I *can* live on for years. The doctor even tells me that I may be able to work again, but I can't imagine that. I was in no way shocked when I heard I had cancer, but I *was* when I heard that one could do something about it, because I had *no* wish to live on. But I couldn't have my wish. I am treated with great kindness by every one & I have an immensely kind doctor who isn't a fool either. I think of you & Lee often with gratitude. Give my good wishes to Doney & my love to Lee.

Affectionately
Ludwig

[1] I received this letter in early December 1949.

45

Strathaird
Lady Mgt. Rd.
Cambridge
11.12.49

My dear Norman,

I want to ask a great favour. It is simply that you do not *under any circumstances* let *any* one know about the nature of my illness who doesn't already know about it. The same goes double for Lee. This is of the greatest importance for me as I plan to go to Vienna for Christmas & *not* to let my family know about the real disease.—von Wright told me that Lee in her great kindness has sent a parcel off for me to Ireland. I'll get it in good time. Thanks for all your kindness (I mean the two of you.). I shall probably not be able to send you a proper X-mas present at all; perhaps a shabby & belated one. Give my love to Lee & to Dr. Mooney[1] & to Doney & Bouwsma.[2] I am slowly getting stronger again.

Affectionately
Ludwig

[1] Dr. Louise Mooney, who treated Wittgenstein in Ithaca. Wittgenstein was very critical of doctors. But he liked Dr. Mooney and thought she was 'really good'.

[2] Oets Bouwsma was Professor of Philosophy at the University of Nebraska. It was Bouwsma who awakened my interest in philosophy when I was a student at Nebraska. We become friends. He was Visiting Professor of Philosophy at Cornell in the summer of 1949 when Wittgenstein was staying in my home. I introduced him to Wittgenstein and he participated in a number of the philosophical discussions with Wittgenstein at Ithaca.

46

IV. Argentinierstr. 16
Wien
Austria
29.12.49.

Dear Norman,

I flew to Vienna on Dec. 24th, which shows you that I am in fairly good health. I am no longer 'despondent', if I ever was. So far I've been very, very lucky. I'm well taken care of here & the food I get is *grand!*—Please see to it that my health is not being unnecessarily discussed; it wouldn't help a bit.—I haven't got any Christmas present for you or Lee. It'll be an Easter present if any.—I found my eldest sister so weak that I can't imagine that she will live many more weeks. She is being taken care of extremely well &

has everything she needs.—The parcel Lee sent to Dublin has arrived there & will be forwarded to me here. I'm sure it's marvellous & much too good for me.—Give all my best wishes to Lee & Ray, & also to Doney & Prof. Bouwsma, & don't forget yourself either.

Affectionately
Ludwig

47   IV. Argentinierstrasse 16
                                           Wien
                                           16.1.50.

Dear Norman,

Thanks for your letter of Dec. 26th. I am very well indeed now & am anything but depressed. I've had *no end* of luck. Even that Dr. Mooney did not recognize my illness was *very* lucky. Give her my love, please.—My brain works very sluggishly these days but I can't say I mind. I'm reading various odds & ends, e.g. Goethe's Theory of colour which, with all its absurdities has very interesting points & stimulates me to think.—I'm sorry you had trouble with the parcel you sent me. It'll teach Lee though not to give me such a lot of good things! At least I hope it will. I'm overeating shamefully as it is & getting more & more fat.—I wish I could again have discussions with you, Doney & Nelson.[1] Give them my good wishes. If we could meet you'd find me pretty slow & stupid; I've only got very few lucid moments. I'm not writing at all because my thoughts never sufficiently crystallize. Not that it matters.

Give my love & *thanks* to Lee. As always, affectionately

Ludwig

Tell Doney his Christmas card wasn't soupy enough.

[1] John Nelson, a postgraduate student of philosophy at Cornell and a friend of mine. I introduced him to Wittgenstein and he participated in some of the discussions. Nelson became a Professor of Philosophy at the University of Colorado, Boulder.

48   IV. Argentinierstrasse 16
                                           Wien
                                           12.2.50.

Dear Norman,

My eldest sister died yesterday. Her end was peaceful & no shock to us as we had expected it for some days.—I intend to stay here for another month. I'm in very good health. So much so that I even had a fairly good discussion with Miss Anscombe a few days ago. I'd be more use to you now than I was last summer in Ithaca.—I'm glad to hear that Lee expects a baby. I *hope* it won't be too difficult for Ray to get readjusted to the new situation; for in such a case the new-comer is apt to attract all affection & the older boy feels out in the cold, rightly or wrongly. Don't tell Ray about this remark which *may* have no application at all in his case.—I can't say that Ryle's book[1] worries me. Perhaps it ought to, but it doesn't. I was interested, however, in what you wrote about it. It tallied with what Smythies & Miss Anscombe told me.—I should like to have discussions with you now. Still, one can't have everything.

Give my love to Lee & my good wishes to all those who don't mind getting them.

Affectionately
Ludwig

[1] *The Concept of Mind* by Gilbert Ryle (Hutchinson's University Library, London, 1949). Ryle was a Professor of Philosophy at Oxford University.

49

c/o v. Wright
Strathaird
Lady Margaret Rd.
Cambridge
5.4.50.

Dear Norman,

I returned from Vienna on March 23rd & came here yesterday. I found Lee's & your lovely Christmas parcel & am enjoying its contents.—I had a letter from Oxford the other day, inviting me to give 6 lectures on philosophy. There are to be lectures of that sort every year by people outside Oxford. The lectures are called John Locke lectures & I'd get £200 for them. I was told, however, that I'd have to expect a large audience, over 200 students & there mustn't be any discussion during the lectures. I haven't yet given them any definite answer but I think I'll reply in the negative. I don't think I can give formal lectures to a large audience that would be any good.—I feel fairly well, though not quite as good as I did in Vienna, & I'm *very* dull & stupid. In this state one shouldn't write letters but I wanted to thank Lee & you for the Christmas parcel & to wish you all a happy Easter. Give my love & good wishes to anyone who has any use for them.

Affectionately
Ludwig

I wish you & I & Doney could again have some discussions!

50   As from Trinity College
                                       Cambridge
                                       17.4.50.

Dear Norman,

Thank you very much for your letter of April 11th. It was very kind of you to take the trouble of approaching a director of the Rockefeller Foundation[1] on my behalf. I will try to tell you as clearly as possible what I think of the matter.

The thought of being able to live where I like, of not having to be a burden or a nuisance to others, of doing philosophy when my nature inclines me to do it is, of course, pleasant for me, as it would be for anyone else who wants to do philosophy. But I could not accept money from the Rockefeller Foundation unless the directors knew the complete truth about me. The truth is this. a) I have not been able to do any sustained good work since the beginning of March 1949. b) Even before that date I could not work *well* for more than 6 or 7 months a year. c) As I'm getting older my thoughts become markedly less forceful & crystallize more rarely & I get tired very much more easily. d) My health is in a somewhat labile state owing to a constant slight anaemia which inclines me to catch infections. This further diminishes the chance of my doing really good work. e) Though it's impossible for me to make any definite predictions, it seems to me likely that my mind will never again work as vigorously as it did, say, 14 months ago. f) I cannot promise to publish anything during my lifetime.

I believe that as long as I live & as often as the state of my mind permits it I will think about philosophical problems & try to write about them. I also believe that much of what I wrote in the past 15 or 20 years may be of interest to people when it's published. But it is, nevertheless, perfectly possible that *all* that I'm *going* to produce will be flat, uninspired & uninteresting. There are many examples of people who did excellent work when they were young, & *very* dull work indeed when they got old.

I think this is all I can say about it. I believe you should show this letter to the director you approached about me. It is obviously impossible to accept a grant under false pretences, & you *may* unintentionally have presented my case in too rosy a light.

My health at present is pretty good. I'm doing some work but I get stuck over simple things & almost all I write is pretty dull. —I may go to Oxford soon & try to live in Miss Anscombe's house. I *like* to stay with the von Wrights but the two children are noisy & I need quiet. I wish I weren't so sensitive!—The address Trinity College will always find me & so, for that matter, will v. Wright's address.

I think I'd better not try to write to you anything about 'motives'[2] today, all the more as I'm not clear about it.

Give my love to Lee.

Affectionately
Ludwig

[1] This was Chadbourne Gilpatrick. I had written to him in the hope of interesting the Foundation in awarding Wittgenstein a research grant. Gilpatrick came to Ithaca to talk with me about it. In January 1951 he went to see Wittgenstein in Oxford to discuss the matter.

[2] In the letter to which Wittgenstein was replying I had, apparently, expressed some philosophical puzzlement about the concept of 'a motive'.

51   27 St. John Street
                                                Oxford
                                                30.7.50.

Dear Norman,
Dear Lee,

I was glad to hear that you had a little boy, chiefly because I imagine that that's what you wanted. If all that's wrong with him is that he looks like Norman, I dare say he'll live that down. May everything go smoothly with him & you & Ray!!—The Rockefeller people didn't write to me, & I don't see that they had any reason; I never wrote to them. Nor could I ever see why they should give me a grant—though it would have been nice if they had done.—I'm pretty well, & I'm working but not particularly well. I get tired soon. The climate here, too, is *very* relaxing. (But I'm not making that responsible.)—As I wrote to you, I planned to go to Norway in August, but I can't go; I *may* go in Autumn. The man with whom I thought of going has to cram for an exam which he failed in July. So may be I'll see Bouwsma when he arrives here in August. I have hardly any philosophical discussions. I could see students if I wanted, but I don't want to. I've got all sorts of unclear thoughts in my old head which perhaps will remain there for ever in this unsatisfactory state. If ever I become clearer again, which is very unlikely, it would be good to have some more talks with you.— Give my good wishes to Doney, if he's still within reach.

Let me hear from you again before long.

As always
Affectionately
Ludwig

P.S. Thanks for the jacket.[1] I'd forgotten all about it & it's mended *beautifully*!

[1] Wittgenstein had left a jacket with us that needed repair. Lee mended it and we posted it to him.

52

27 St. John Street
Oxford
1.12.50.

Dear Norman,

Thanks for your letter of Nov. 3rd. I found it when I came back from Norway about 10 days ago. I was away 5 weeks & before that I was illish for about a month. In Norway the friend who went with me fell ill with bronchitis *twice*. So there was no end of trouble & I postponed writing to my friends from one day to the other. This doesn't mean that we didn't enjoy our journey, for we *did*, & we had wonderful weather. I had intended to do some work but I didn't do any. I may possibly go back to Norway before long & try to work. It's the only place I know where I can have real quiet. Of course it's possible that I'm no longer able to do any decent research, but it's certainly worth while finding out if I am or not. Please don't talk about this plan of mine for the present. I haven't yet decided, & although several people know of it, there are others I don't want to know.

I have given Miss Anscombe, Smythies & Bouwsma your kind regards. It's always *very* pleasant to see Bouwsma. He & his wife are such kind & natural people. I am very glad that he sees Smythies regularly; I can't imagine that he sees many people in this place worth seeing. He also has had a good many discussions with Miss A . . . You're quite right, a mathematician by name of Turing[1] attended my lectures in '39 (they were *pretty* poor!) & it's probably the same man who wrote the article you mention.[2] I haven't read it but I imagine it's *no* leg-pull. Von Wright is in Finland & is coming back to Cambridge in January. I don't know if I shall see him. I saw my doctor there the other day & looked up Moore. He seemed pretty well but says he must take it very easy because of his heart.

Give my love to Lee & remember me to Doney & Dr. Mooney. I should very much like to see them again though it's very unlikely that I will.

My health is not too bad but I am very dull & stupid indeed (as this letter shows).

Affectionately
Ludwig

[1] A. M. Turing, a mathematical logician, attended Wittgenstein's lectures on the philosophy of mathematics in 1939.

[2] The article I had read, and of which I wondered whether it was a 'leg-pull', was Turing's 'Computing Machinery and Intelligence', published in *Mind* 1950. Turing proposed a test for determining whether a machine has successfully simulated human intelligent behaviour. His article gave rise to much subsequent discussion by philosophers of 'the Turing test' or 'Turing game'.

53   27 St. John Street
Oxford
2.1.51.

Dear Norman,
Dear Lee,

Thank you very, very much for the wonderful Christmas present. I have the pull-over on right now & am looking very distinguished in it.—I don't know if I wrote to you that when I was in Norway in October I thought of going back there to do some work. I asked a friend there who has a farm could I come back & stay over the winter, or longer. I was told that I could. It would have been a *very* cheap & very quiet place. I booked a passage on a steamer Newcastle–Bergen on Dec. 30th. Shortly before Christmas I heard that my friend could not put me up after all & at the same time I fell ill & so couldn't have gone anyway. I'm very much better now & I'm waiting for some news from some other people in Norway to whom I wrote, asking them if they knew a suitable place for me. So far I haven't heard from them & I'm *not* optimistic. I spent Christmas in Cambridge in my doctor's house. I'd gone to see him to have an examination before travelling to Norway & I fell ill in his house & had to stay there. Yesterday I came back here & found your lovely present & Xmas card. In Cambridge I read a book which interested me & which I thought was rather well written. It's called 'Rommel' by an English Brigadier Young & is a kind of biography of the German general & a history of his exploits. I thought it might be a possible, though very belated, Christmas present & I'm sending it to you. It's possible that you won't like it at all.

All good wishes, as always, & thanks again.

Affectionately
Ludwig

54   27 St. John Street
                                                      Oxford
                                                      12.1.51.

Dear Norman,

Thank you for your letter & the 2 pictures. Both of them are *very* good.—Yesterday a Mr. Gilpatrick from the Rockefeller Foundation visited me. I told him what I wrote to you some months ago, i.e., that in my present state of health & intellectual dullness I couldn't accept a grant; but I said that if, against all probability & hope, I should one day find that I could again do worthwhile work in philosophy, I'd write to him. And so we parted on friendly terms.—The Bouwsmas are enormously kind to me. I am ever so glad that he can have discussions with Smythies & Miss A. Otherwise this place is a philosophical desert; & I am just good enough to eat apple sauce with a philosopher.[1] My mind's completely dead. This isn't a complaint, for I don't really suffer from it. I know that life must have an end once & that mental life can cease before the rest does.—Your pullover is wonderful & fits me perfectly.

Give my love to Lee & good luck to Ray.

Thanks for all your kindness.

Affectionately
Ludwig

From Bouwsma & Gilpatrick I heard that you gave a good paper at Toronto.

---

[1] The Bouwsmas, who were spending the year in Oxford, often invited Wittgenstein to meals. He was extremely fond of Mrs. Bouwsma's home-made apple sauce.

55   'Storeys End'
                                                 Storeys Way
                                                 Cambridge
                                                 Today. (That's all I know)[1]

My dear Norman,

Thanks for your letter of Feb. 6th. As you see I'm in Cambridge;
I'm staying with my doctor[2] who is an extremely kind man & an
excellent doctor. I also saw a specialist here & I'm to have deep X-
ray treatment again, this time for my spine. I've had a pretty bad
time at Oxford but am feeling much better now (for reasons no one
knows), I have very little pain & discomfort.—Yes, the Bouwsmas
were *angelic* & so was Miss Anscombe. I'm not sure how long I
shall stay here. It'll depend on how things go.—I believe I wrote to
you that before I fell ill I intended to go to Norway to TRY to work
there. I'd even taken a ticket to Bergen. I don't know if I'll ever get
well enough to do this; probably not. In this case I shall probably go
back to Oxford from here. I can't even *think* of work at present, &
it doesn't matter, if only I don't live too long! I'm not depressed
though. von Wright came to see me twice. If he knew I was writing
to you he'd send you his very best wishes & so would Smythies &
Miss Anscombe.

I wish I could have a talk again with you, Doney & Nelson. But
even if I could be with you you'd find that my head was empty. (It
was half empty already when I was in Ithaca.) Please give my kind
regards to D. & N. & to Dr. Mooney. I like to think of her & I
always praise her when I talk of her.—Give my love to L. & R. &
C.[3]
                                       As always, affectionately
                                                 Ludwig

[1] Probably written in February 1951.
[2] Dr. Edward Bevan invited Wittgenstein to live until his death with him and
Mrs. Bevan (Memoir, p. 80).
[2] Lee, Ray, and our infant son Christopher.

56   76 Storeys Way
                                                 Cambridge
                                                 19.3.51.

Dear Norman,

Thanks for your letter. I'm feeling much better now than I did a
month ago. I have hardly any pain. The improvement is probably
due to the deep X-ray treatment I took for a few weeks. (This time

it wasn't my shoulders but my spine that got the rays). I am of course very weak & there seems no doubt that this isn't going to change for the better as time goes on. I hardly think that I'll be on this earth when you come to Cambridge in Autumn '52. Still, one doesn't know.

I am not depressed in the least, by the way.—I'm very glad you liked the Rommel book. I looked at it quite recently again & was impressed again by the thoroughly *decent* way in which it's written. Such books are few & far between. The author, where he disagrees with other people of high rank (as p.p. 160–161), expresses himself very cautiously, but one always knows what he thinks & what he would say if he could let himself go:—I can see that the question of what to do with Ray while you're in England is serious & I can't suggest anything at all. But there's still plenty of time to think about it. I'm glad that v. Wright proposed you. He told me about it a few weeks ago.—In a way it might be good to bring Ray to Europe (though not to enter him in a school) because it might open his eyes. But on the other hand it might shut them, & so I just don't know at all.—I saw Moore yesterday & we talked philosophy. But it was no good because I was far too dull & hazy. When I'm alone I am sometimes a bit brighter.—The other day I saw a laudatory review of two philosophical books in the 'New Statesman'. One was by a man ——, who came to my classes while you were in Cambridge, I think; the other seemed to contain articles by ——, ——, —— & other charlatans. The review I read particularly praised one remark of ——'s which came straight out of my lectures. I'd like to see a review some day which debunks these people.

Give my love to Lee & all my best wishes to everybody who can make use of them.

Affectionately
Ludwig

57

76 Storeys Way
Cambridge
16.4.51.

Dear Norman,

Thanks for your letter. Apart from a certain weakness which has constant ups & downs I'm feeling *very* well these days. My room here is much more agreeable than the one in Oxford. Not that anyone could *possibly* be kinder to me than Miss Anscombe was; & I was very happy there, too, while I was ill. But now that I'm up the whole day I prefer it here. Thanks for sending me the book Kon-tiki.[1] I've often heard of it & it's bound to be interesting.—I saw Moore twice recently & had discussions with him. One very bad one, the other fairly good. I was responsible for the bad one's being bad. An extraordinary thing has happened to me. About a month ago I suddenly found myself in the right frame of mind for doing philosophy. I had been *absolutely* certain that I'd never again be able to do it. It's the first time after more than 2 years that the curtain in my brain has gone up.—Of course, so far I've only worked for about 5 weeks & it may be all over by tomorrow, but it bucks me up a lot now.

I'm indoors most of the time, all the more as the weather is pretty rotten & *very* cold, but I can go out for short strolls.—I want to go to Oxford before long to visit Smythies & Bouwsma if all goes well with me.

Miss Anscombe sends her good wishes. Give my love to everybody.

Affectionately
Ludwig

Remember me to Dr. Mooney. I like to think of her.

[1] *Kon-Tiki: Across the Pacific by Raft*, by Thor Heyerdahl, translation by F. H. Lyon (Rand McNally & Co., Chicago, 1950).

This was my last letter from Wittgenstein. It was written thirteen days before his death.

INDEX